GRADE

D0889456

A BALANCED MATHEMATICS PROGRAM INTEGRATING SCIENCE AND LANGUAGE ARTS

Unit Resource Guide
Unit 11

Number Patterns, Primes, and Fractions

THIRD EDITION

KENDALL/HUNT PUBLISHING COMPANY
4050 Westmark Drive   Dubuque, Iowa 52002

A TIMS® Curriculum
University of Illinois at Chicago

UIC The University of Illinois
at Chicago

The original edition was based on work supported by the National Science Foundation under grant No. MDR 9050226 and the University of Illinois at Chicago. Any opinions, findings, and conclusions or recommendations expressed in this publication are those of the author(s) and do not necessarily reflect the views of the granting agencies.

Printed in the United States of America

1 2 3 4 5 6 7 8 9 10   11 10 09 08 07

Letter Home

Number Patterns, Primes, and Fractions

Date: _____

Dear Family Member:

During this unit, your child will explore patterns in our number system, describe the patterns, and use them to solve problems. This kind of work is similar to the work mathematicians often do. We will investigate factors, multiples, primes, and square numbers. Your child will use concrete objects, paper and pencil activities, and a game to help understand how numbers are related. These activities will help with addition, subtraction, multiplication, and division of whole numbers and fractions.

Playing the game *Factor 40* helps students learn how numbers are related.

You can help your child by:

- Playing the game *Factor 40* with your child after he or she has played it at school.

- Asking your child to explain prime numbers, factors, multiples, and square numbers.

Thank you for your cooperation.

Sincerely,

_____

Carta al hogar

Patrones numéricos, números primos y fracciones

Fecha: _____

Estimado miembro de familia:

Durante esta unidad, su hijo/a investigará los patrones del sistema numérico, describirá los patrones y los usará para resolver problemas. Esta clase de trabajo es semejante al trabajo que suelen hacer los matemáticos. Investigaremos los factores, los múltiplos, los números primos y los números al cuadrado. Su hijo/a usará objetos concretos, actividades con papel y lápiz, y un juego para ayudarle a entender cómo se relacionan los números. Estas actividades ayudarán a su hijo/a con la suma, la resta, la multiplicación y la división de números enteros y fracciones.

Jugar al juego *Factor 40* ayuda a los estudiantes a aprender cómo se relacionan los números.

Usted puede ayudar a su hijo de la siguiente manera:

• Jugando el juego *Factor 40* con su hijo/a después de que lo haya jugado en la escuela.

• Pidiéndole a su hijo/a que le explique los números primos, los factores, los múltiplos y los números al cuadrado.

Gracias por su cooperación.

Atentamente,

_____

Table of Contents

Unit 11
Number Patterns, Primes, and Fractions

Unit 11

Outline
Number Patterns, Primes, and Fractions

Unit Summary

Estimated Class Sessions **11-14**

Students investigate some of the underlying structures of arithmetic, often referred to as number theory. They play a game in which they must find all the factors of the numbers from one to forty. They identify prime and composite numbers using a 100 chart and a process developed by Eratosthenes, a famous Greek mathematician. They then examine and describe patterns in the chart. Students complete an assessment activity, *A Further Look at Patterns and Primes,* using the same process on a different chart. In a different activity, students investigate patterns in square numbers. In the latter part of the unit, students use common factors and common multiples to rename, compare, and reduce fractions.

Major Concept Focus

- factors
- multiples
- Sieve of Eratosthenes
- exponents
- prime factorization
- common denominators
- comparing fractions
- adding and subtracting fractions
- number patterns
- prime numbers
- composite numbers
- factor trees
- square numbers
- reducing fractions to lowest terms
- point graphs
- communicating mathematically
- Student Rubric: *Telling*

Pacing Suggestions

This unit is designed to be completed in 11 to 14 days. Students discover patterns and relationships among numbers as they investigate prime and composite numbers.

- Part 2 of Lesson 3 *Patterns with Square Numbers* is optional. Use these Challenge Questions as an extension.

- Lesson 8 *From Factors to Fractions* is an optional lesson in which students solve multistep problems. You can assign these problems for homework. They are also appropriate for use by a substitute teacher since preparation is minimal.

Assessment Indicators

Use the following Assessment Indicators and the *Observational Assessment Record* that follows the Background section in this unit to assess students on key ideas.

A1. Can students find all the factors of a number?

A2. Can students identify prime, composite, and square numbers?

A3. Can students find the prime factorization of a number?

A4. Can students reduce fractions to lowest terms?

A5. Can students find common denominators?

A6. Can students compare fractions?

A7. Can students add and subtract fractions using common denominators?

A8. Can students use variables in formulas?

A9. Can students identify and describe number patterns?

Unit Planner

	Lesson Information	Supplies	Copies/Transparencies

Lesson 1

Factor 40

URG Pages 23–35
SG Pages 348–352
DAB Page 181

DPP A–D
HP Part 1

Estimated Class Sessions
2

Game
Students play *Factor 40* to review factors. They review prime numbers and composite numbers.

Homework
1. Assign the Homework section in the *Student Guide.*
2. Assign Part 1 of the Home Practice.

Assessment
1. Use homework *Questions 6–8* as an assessment.
2. Use the *Observational Assessment Record* to note students' abilities to find all the factors of a number.

• 1 calculator per student

• 4 copies of *Three-column Data Table* URG Page 32 per student, optional

• 1 transparency of *Factor 40 Game Board* DAB Page 181

• 1 copy of *Observational Assessment Record* URG Pages 11–12 to be used throughout this unit

---

Lesson 2

Sifting for Primes

URG Pages 36–43
SG Pages 353–355
DAB Page 183

DPP E–F
HP Part 2

Estimated Class Sessions
1

Activity
Students use the Sieve of Eratosthenes to find the prime numbers from 1 to 100. Students look for patterns and sift for prime numbers from 101–200.

Math Facts
DPP Bit E reviews the division facts for the 3s and 9s.

Homework
1. Students sift for the prime numbers from 101 to 200 on the *200 Chart* Activity Page in the *Discovery Assignment Book.*
2. Assign Part 2 of the Home Practice.

Assessment
Use the *Observational Assessment Record* to note students' abilities to identify prime numbers.

• 1–4 transparencies of *200 Chart* DAB Page 183, optional

Lesson 3

Patterns with Square Numbers

URG Pages 44–56
SG Pages 356–359

DPP G–J

Estimated Class Sessions
2

Activity
Students develop a visual picture of square numbers. Students discover a relationship between square numbers and odd numbers.

Math Facts
DPP item I reviews the division facts for the 3s and 9s.

• 25 square-inch tiles per student

• 1 copy of *Three-column Data Table* URG Page 32 per student

• 1 copy of *Centimeter Grid Paper* URG Page 53 per student

• 1 copy of *Centimeter Graph Paper* URG Page 54 per student

• 1 transparency of *Three-column Data Table* URG Page 32, optional

• 1 transparency of *Centimeter Grid Paper* URG Page 53

• 1 transparency of *Centimeter Graph Paper* URG Page 54, optional

	Lesson Information	Supplies	Copies/ Transparencies
Lesson 4 **Finding Prime Factors** URG Pages 57–67 SG Pages 360–362 DAB Page 185 DPP K–L HP Part 3 *Estimated Class Sessions* **1-2**	**Activity** Students build factor trees of numbers using their calculators. Students write numbers as products of primes using exponents. **Homework** Assign *Questions 1–4* in the Homework section in the *Student Guide*. **Assessment** Use Part 3 of the Home Practice to assess students' fluency with factors, exponents, and prime numbers.	• 1 calculator per student	• 2–3 blank transparencies, optional
Lesson 5 **Comparing Fractions** URG Pages 68–77 SG Pages 363–367 DPP M–P HP Part 5 *Estimated Class Sessions* **2**	**Activity** Students compare fractions using common denominators. **Math Facts** DPP items M and P include a review of the division facts for the 3s and 9s. **Homework** 1. Assign the questions in the Homework section. 2. Assign Part 5 of the Home Practice. **Assessment** 1. Use DPP Task P as a quiz. 2. Use the *Observational Assessment Record* to note students' abilities to find common denominators and to compare fractions.		
Lesson 6 **Reducing Fractions** URG Pages 78–88 SG Pages 82 & 368–372 DPP Q–R HP Parts 4 & 6 *Estimated Class Sessions* **1-2**	**Activity** Students use common factors to reduce fractions to lowest terms. Students add and subtract fractions after finding common denominators, and they solve division problems whose quotients are mixed numbers. They then reduce answers to lowest terms. **Math Facts** DPP item Q reviews the division facts for the 3s and 9s. **Homework** 1. Assign the problems in the Homework section of the *Reducing Fractions* Activity Pages. 2. Assign Parts 4 and 6 of the Home Practice. **Assessment** Students complete the *Skills Check-Up* Assessment Page.		• 1 copy of *Skills Check-Up* URG Page 84 per student

(Continued)

	Lesson Information	Supplies	Copies/Transparencies

Lesson 7

A Further Look at Patterns and Primes

URG Pages 89–100

DPP S–V

Estimated Class Sessions

2

Assessment Activity
Students use different colors to sift for prime numbers using a six-column 100 chart. Students write about the patterns they see in the completed chart. Included are patterns involving multiples, prime numbers, and factors.

Math Facts
DPP items S and U review math facts.

Homework
Assign some or all of the word problems in Lesson 8 as homework.

Assessment
1. Have students put their work for this activity in their collection folders for possible inclusion in their portfolios.
2. Use the *Observational Assessment Record* to note students' abilities to identify and describe number patterns. Transfer your observations to students' *Individual Assessment Record Sheets.*

Supplies:
• 4 different-colored crayons per student

Copies/Transparencies:
• 1 copy of *A Further Look at Patterns and Primes* URG Page 98 per student
• 1 copy of *6-column 100 Chart* URG Page 99 per student
• 1 copy of *TIMS Multidimensional Rubric* TIG, Assessment section
• 1 copy of *Individual Assessment Record Sheet* TIG, Assessment section per student, previously copied for use throughout the year
• 1 transparency or poster of Student Rubric: *Telling* TIG, Assessment section, optional

Lesson 8

From Factors to Fractions

URG Pages 101–104
SG Page 373

Estimated Class Sessions

1

OPTIONAL LESSON

Optional Activity
Students solve word problems using fractions and decimals.

Homework
Assign some or all of the problems for homework.

Supplies:
• 1 calculator per student

Connections

A current list of literature and software connections is available at *www.mathtrailblazers.com*. You can also find information on connections in the *Teacher Implementation Guide* Literature List and Software List sections.

Literature Connections

Suggested Titles

- Dahl, Roald. *Esio Trot.* Puffin Books, New York, 1999.
- Hulme, Joy N. *Sea Squares.* Hyperion Books for Children, New York, 1993. (Lesson 3)
- Sachar, Louis. *Sideways Arithmetic from Wayside School.* Scholastic Press, New York, 1989.

Software Connections

- *Fraction Attraction* develops understanding of fractions using fraction bars, pie charts, hundreds blocks, and other materials.
- *Graph Master* allows students to collect data and create their own graphs.
- *Math Munchers Deluxe* provides practice in basic facts and finding equivalent fractions, decimals, percents, ratios, angles and identifying geometric shapes, factors, and multiples in an arcade-like game.
- *Math Mysteries: Advanced Fractions* develops multistep problem solving with fractions.
- *Mighty Math Number Heroes* poses short answer questions about fractions, number operations, polygons, and probability.
- *Tenth Planet: Fraction Operations* develops conceptual understanding of fraction operations, including finding common denominators.

Teaching All Math Trailblazers Students

Math Trailblazers® lessons are designed for students with a wide range of abilities. The lessons are flexible and do not require significant adaptation for diverse learning styles or academic levels. However, when needed, lessons can be tailored to allow students to engage their abilities to the greatest extent possible while building knowledge and skills.

To assist you in meeting the needs of all students in your classroom, this section contains information about some of the features in the curriculum that allow all students access to mathematics. For additional information, see the Teaching the *Math Trailblazers* Student: Meeting Individual Needs section in the *Teacher Implementation Guide.*

Differentiation Opportunities in this Unit

Games

Use games to promote or extend understanding of math concepts and to practice skills with children who need more practice.

- Lesson 1 *Factor 40*

Journal Prompts

Journal prompts provide opportunities for students to explain and reflect on mathematical problems. They can help both students who need practice explaining their ideas and students who benefit from answering higher order questions. Students with various learning styles can express themselves using pictures, words, and sentences. Teachers can alter journal prompts to suit students' ability levels. The following lesson contains a journal prompt:

- Lesson 1 *Factor 40*

DPP Challenges

DPP Challenges are items from the Daily Practice and Problems that usually take more than fifteen minutes to complete. These problems are more thought-provoking and can be used to stretch students' problem-solving skills. The following lessons have DPP Challenges in them:

- DPP Challenge D from Lesson 1 *Factor 40*
- DPP Challenge J from Lesson 3 *Patterns with Square Numbers*
- DPP Challenge V from Lesson 7 *A Further Look at Patterns and Primes*

Extensions

Use extensions to enrich lessons. Many extensions provide opportunities to further involve or challenge students of all abilities. Take a moment to review the extensions prior to beginning this unit. Some extensions may require additional preparation and planning. The following lessons contain extensions:

- Lesson 1 *Factor 40*
- Lesson 3 *Patterns with Square Numbers*
- Lesson 6 *Reducing Fractions*
- Lesson 7 *A Further Look at Patterns and Primes*

Background
Number Patterns, Primes, and Fractions

In this unit students investigate some of the underlying structures of arithmetic, often referred to as number theory. Number theory is a branch of mathematics that investigates prime and composite numbers, factors, multiples, and many interesting number patterns. Students need to develop an understanding of the properties of numbers to build a foundation for using numbers in addition, subtraction, multiplication, and division with whole numbers, fractions, and decimals.

Prime and Composite Numbers

In Lessons 1–4 students learn about prime and composite numbers (numbers with more than 2 distinct factors) and patterns associated with these numbers. The study of patterns helps students make generalizations about numbers. Investigating number patterns is an ongoing part of the curriculum. Students are somewhat familiar with the concepts in this unit, as they were introduced in earlier grades. Students began looking at patterns in multiplication and division in third grade. These concepts were extended in Unit 4 of fourth grade as students explored multiples and factors. Students were also introduced to the prime factorization of a number using factor trees. This unit pulls together and expands on this earlier work.

Fractions

Investigations in this unit offer insights into how whole numbers relate to fractions. In Lessons 5 and 6, students use common factors and common multiples to rename, compare, and order fractions. Students were introduced to these ideas in earlier units using pattern blocks and rectangles on dot paper. In this unit, students manipulate fractions without concrete or pictorial representations. However, these tools should be available for use when necessary.

As students study the properties of numbers and relationships among numbers, they come to understand mathematics as a cohesive body of knowledge and not a collection of isolated facts and rules. They can more easily apply their understanding and skills to new tasks. This provides a foundation for problem solving, where the focus is on the use of numbers in problems in which there are a variety of solutions or solution paths.

Resources

- Burns, Marilyn. *About Teaching Mathematics. A K–8 Resource.* Math Solutions Publications, White Plains, NY, 1992.
- Burns, Marilyn. *The I Hate Mathematics! Book.* Scholastic, Inc., New York, 1975.
- Cuevas, Gilbert J., and Karol Yeatts. *Navigating Through Algebra in Grades 3–5.* National Council of Teachers of Mathematics, Reston, VA, 2001.
- Eves, Howard. *An Introduction to the History of Mathematics.* Holt, Rinehart and Winston, New York, 1969.
- *Grolier Encyclopedia on CD-ROM.* Grolier Electronic Publishing, Inc., 1995.
- Phillips, Elizabeth, et al. *Patterns and Functions* from the Curriculum and Evaluation Standards Addenda Series, Grades 5–8. National Council of Teachers of Mathematics, Reston, VA, 1992.
- *Principles and Standards for School Mathematics.* National Council of Teachers of Mathematics, Reston, VA, 2000.
- Serifina, Rachael, Elden Cann, David Lavoie. "Prime Number Chart." *Teaching Children Mathematics.* pp. 203–204. November, 1995.

- Sowder, Judith. "Estimation and Number Sense." In *Handbook of Research on Mathematics Teaching and Learning,* D.A. Grouws (ed.), pp. 371–389. Macmillan Publishing Company, New York, 1992.

- Tahan, Malba (translated by Leslie Clark and Alastair Reid). *The Man Who Counted.* W.W. Norton & Company, Inc., New York, 1993.

- West, Beverly Henderson, Ellen Norma Griesbach, Jerry Duncan Taylor, Louise Todd Taylor. (eds.) *The Prentice-Hall Encyclopedia of Mathematics.* Prentice-Hall, Inc., Upper Saddle River, NJ, 1982.

Observational Assessment Record

(A1) Can students find all the factors of a number?

(A2) Can students identify prime, composite, and square numbers?

(A3) Can students find the prime factorization of a number?

(A4) Can students reduce fractions to lowest terms?

(A5) Can students find common denominators?

(A6) Can students compare fractions?

(A7) Can students add and subtract fractions using common denominators?

(A8) Can students use variables in formulas?

(A9) Can students identify and describe number patterns?

(A10) _____

Name	A1	A2	A3	A4	A5	A6	A7	A8	A9	A10	Comments
1.											
2.											
3.											
4.											
5.											
6.											
7.											
8.											
9.											
10.											
11.											
12.											
13.											

Name	A1	A2	A3	A4	A5	A6	A7	A8	A9	A10	Comments
14.											
15.											
16.											
17.											
18.											
19.											
20.											
21.											
22.											
23.											
24.											
25.											
26.											
27.											
28.											
29.											
30.											
31.											
32.											

Unit 11

Daily Practice and Problems
Number Patterns, Primes, and Fractions

A DPP Menu for Unit 11

Two Daily Practice and Problems (DPP) items are included for each class session listed in the Unit Outline. A scope and sequence chart for the DPP is in the *Teacher Implementation Guide.*

Icons in the Teacher Notes column designate the subject matter of each DPP item. The first item in each class session is always a Bit and the second is either a Task or Challenge. Each item falls into one or more of the categories listed below. A menu of the DPP items for Unit 11 follows.

N Number Sense	Computation	Time	Geometry
C, H–M, O–R, T	A, B, F, I, K, M, N, P–R, T, U	B	D
Math Facts	$ Money	Measurement	Data
E, I, M, P, Q, S, U	F		D, G, V

The *Daily Practice and Problems and Home Practice Guide* in the *Teacher Implementation Guide* includes information on how and when to use the DPP.

Review of Math Facts

By the end of fourth grade, students in *Math Trailblazers* are expected to demonstrate fluency with all the division facts. The DPP for this unit continues the systematic approach to reviewing the division facts. This unit reviews the 3s and 9s.

For more information about the distribution and assessment of the math facts, see the TIMS Tutor: *Math Facts* in the *Teacher Implementation Guide.*

 **Daily Practice and Problems**

Students may solve the items individually, in groups, or as a class. The items may also be assigned for homework. The DPPs are also available on the Teacher Resource CD.

Student Questions	Teacher Notes

 Multiplication and Division

Solve each problem using paper and pencil.

A. $234 \times 6 =$ B. $24{,}000 \div 60 =$

C. $26 \times 14 =$ D. $903 \div 7 =$

TIMS Bit

A. 1404

B. 400

C. 364

D. 129

Remind students to use efficient methods. Note that they can solve B using mental math.

 Parent-Teacher Conferences

Mr. Moreno plans to meet with the parents of each of his 22 students during Parent-Teacher Conferences. The conferences are held from 4:00 to 6:00 P.M. and from 7:00 to 9:00 P.M. (There is a one hour dinner break for the teachers from 6:00 to 7:00.)

1. About how long can Mr. Moreno meet with the parents of each student, if they all plan to come to the conferences?

2. Mr. Moreno finds out that 2 parents are unable to attend the conferences. Eight parents need to come between 7:00 and 9:00 because of their work schedules. The rest of the parents will come between 4 and 6 o'clock. Help Mr. Moreno schedule his conferences.

TIMS Task

1. About 10–11 minutes.

2. Mr. Moreno should schedule fifteen minute conferences between 7:00 and 9:00 to accommodate the 8 parents. Twelve parents plan to come between 4:00 and 6:00. He should plan 10 minute conferences with each of these parents.

C Less Than One

Without a calculator, decide which of the following products are less than one. Explain your reasoning.

A. $7.32 \times 0.5 =$

B. $2.36 \times 0.04 =$

C. $180.3 \times 0.002 =$

TIMS Bit

Some possible explanations:

A. 0.5 is the same as $\frac{1}{2}$. One-half of 7.32 would be close to $3\frac{1}{2}$, so the answer will be greater than 1.

B. One half (or 0.50) of 2.36 is approximately 1; $\frac{4}{100}$ is much smaller than 0.50, so the answer will be less than 1.

C. The answer should be close to 0 since $0.001 \times 180 = 0.180$.

D Coordinated Coordinates

Use a sheet of graph paper to help you with this problem. Write down some ordered pairs in which the x-coordinates are equal in value to the y-coordinates. Plot the points and describe the resulting graph. Filling in this table first may help.

x	y
2	2
-2	-2

TIMS Challenge

The points on the graph will form a straight line passing through zero equidistant to the x and y axes.

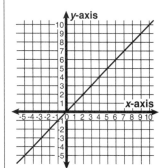

E Division Practice I

A. $72 \div 9 =$ B. $24 \div 3 =$

C. $45 \div 9 =$ D. $15 \div 3 =$

E. $36 \div 9 =$ F. $12 \div 3 =$

TIMS Bit

A. 8   B. 8

C. 5   D. 5

E. 4   F. 4

F Hawaii for Half

A travel agent offers Maria a 50% discount on a trip to Hawaii. The trip includes airfare and 11 nights in a hotel. The price for the trip before the discount is $3038. If the airfare will cost Maria $650, what is the cost of the hotel per night after the discount?

TIMS Task

$79 per night (3038 ÷ 2 = 1519—Maria's cost. Then, 1519 − 650 = $869—cost of hotel; $869 ÷ 11 nights = $79/night)

G What's the Probability?

Lin rolls a number cube. The six faces show the numbers 1, 2, 3, 4, 5, and 6. The probability that she will roll an even number is $\frac{3}{6}$ (or $\frac{1}{2}$) since she has 3 ways (2, 4, 6) to roll an even number out of 6 possible numbers. What is the probability that she will roll:

A. a prime number?

B. a factor of 6?

TIMS Bit

A. $\frac{3}{6} = \frac{1}{2}$ (2, 3, and 5 are prime numbers)

B. $\frac{4}{6} = \frac{2}{3}$ (1, 2, 3, and 6 are factors of 6)

H Decimals to Fractions

Express the following decimals as fractions. Reduce the fractions to lowest terms.

A. 0.25   B. 0.6

C. 0.35   D. 0.004

E. 0.068   F. 0.128

TIMS Task

A. $\frac{25}{100} = \frac{1}{4}$

B. $\frac{6}{10} = \frac{3}{5}$

C. $\frac{35}{100} = \frac{7}{20}$

D. $\frac{4}{1000} = \frac{1}{250}$

E. $\frac{68}{1000} = \frac{17}{250}$

F. $\frac{128}{1000} = \frac{16}{125}$

Division Practice II

TIMS Bit

A. 810 ÷ 90 =   B. 300 ÷ 30 =

C. 6300 ÷ 70 =   D. 180 ÷ 20 =

E. 2100 ÷ 70 =   F. 6000 ÷ 20 =

G. 900 ÷ 30 =   H. 900 ÷ 10 =

I. 540 ÷ 90 =

A. 9   B. 10

C. 90   D. 9

E. 30   F. 300

G. 30   H. 90

I. 6

J **Prime Factors**

TIMS Challenge

Use the Sieve of Eratosthenes to find all the prime numbers between 301 and 320. Use your calculator as needed.

301	302	303	304	305
306	307	308	309	310
311	312	313	314	315
316	317	318	319	320

307, 311, 313, 317

K **Division**

TIMS Bit

Solve using paper and pencil. Estimate to be sure your answers are reasonable.

1. 5600 ÷ 80 =

2. 5973 ÷ 78 =

3. 48,000 ÷ 60 =

4. 47,346 ÷ 61 =

1. 70

2. 76 R45

3. 800

4. 776 R10

Divisibility Rules

Tell which numbers below are divisible by 2.
Tell which numbers below are divisible by 3.
Remember, a number is divisible by 3 if the
sum of its digits is divisible by 3.

A. 26   B. 258

C. 368   D. 939

E. 1032

Which numbers above are divisible by 6?
Write the divisibility rule for 6.

TIMS Task

Students explored divisibility rules
in Grade 4 Unit 7. Students can also
use their calculators to test
divisibility.

A. 2   B. 2 and 3

C. 2   D. 3

E. 2 and 3

Both 258 and 1032 are divisible by
6. A number that is divisible by 2
and 3 is also divisible by 6.

 **Division Practice III**

A. $180 \div 6 =$

B. $270 \div 3 =$

C. $4500 \div 50 =$

D. $2400 \div 800 =$

E. $36,000 \div 40 =$

F. $90,000 \div 100 =$

TIMS Bit

A. 30

B. 90

C. 90

D. 3

E. 900

F. 900

N **Practicing the Operations**

Solve the following problems using a paper-
and-pencil method. Estimate to be sure your
answers are reasonable.

1. A. $34 \times 93 =$ B. $3489 \div 13 =$

   C. $423 \times 9 =$ D. $0.43 \times 0.7 =$

   E. $0.23 \times 8 =$ F. $6086 \div 39 =$

2. Explain your estimation strategy for E.

TIMS Task

Discuss students' estimation
strategies.

1. A. 3162   B. 268 R5

   C. 3807   D. 0.301

   E. 1.84   F. 156 R2

2. Possible strategy:
   0.23 is about 0.25 or $\frac{1}{4}$.
   $\frac{1}{4}$ of 8 is 2.

Student Questions	Teacher Notes

Fractions

Find one number for *n* that makes each sentence true.

A. $\frac{1}{5} = \frac{n}{25}$

B. $\frac{6}{21} = \frac{2}{n}$

C. $\frac{n}{12} < \frac{3}{4}$

D. $\frac{7}{8} < \frac{n}{16}$

TIMS Bit

A. $\frac{1}{5} = \frac{5}{25}$

B. $\frac{6}{21} = \frac{2}{7}$

C. Answers will vary. Since $\frac{9}{12} = \frac{3}{4}$, any numerator less than 9 will make the sentence true.

D. Answers will vary. Since $\frac{7}{8} = \frac{14}{16}$, any numerator greater than 14 will make the sentence true.

Ⓟ Finding Factors

1. Find all the factors for the following numbers. Tell which numbers are prime.

   A. 23

   B. 258

   C. 39

   D. 73

   E. 1278

2. Draw a factor tree for each composite number above. Then write its prime factorization.

TIMS Task

1. A. 1, 23; prime

   B. 1, 2, 3, 6, 43, 86, 129, 258

   C. 1, 3, 13, 39

   D. 1, 73; prime

   E. 1, 2, 3, 6, 9, 18, 71, 142, 213, 426, 639, 1278

2. A. prime

   B. $2 \times 3 \times 43$

   C. 3×13

   D. prime

   E. $2 \times 3^2 \times 71$

Ⓠ Division Fact Practice IV

A. $630 \div n = 7$

B. $n \div 300 = 7$

C. $5400 \div n = 90$

D. $27,000 \div 30 = n$

E. $8100 \div 900 = n$

F. $1800 \div n = 600$

TIMS Bit

A. 90

B. 2100

C. 60

D. 900

E. 9

F. 3

| | Student Questions | Teacher Notes |

 More Fractions

1. Rewrite each fraction as a mixed number. Write all fractions in lowest terms.

   A. $\frac{78}{8}$

   B. $\frac{58}{12}$

   C. $\frac{69}{15}$

2. Solve the following. Reduce your answers to lowest terms. Estimate to be sure your answers are reasonable.

   A. $\frac{5}{18} + \frac{1}{6} =$

   B. $\frac{4}{5} - \frac{3}{10} =$

   C. $\frac{1}{2} - \frac{1}{30} =$

TIMS Task

1. A. $9\frac{6}{8} = 9\frac{3}{4}$
   B. $4\frac{10}{12} = 4\frac{5}{6}$
   C. $4\frac{9}{15} = 4\frac{3}{5}$
2. A. $\frac{8}{18} = \frac{4}{9}$
   B. $\frac{5}{10} = \frac{1}{2}$
   C. $\frac{14}{30} = \frac{7}{15}$

 Practice: 3s and 9s

A. $30 \div 3 =$ B. $45 \div 5 =$

C. $90 \div 10 =$ D. $18 \div 6 =$

E. $24 \div 8 =$ F. $9 \div 3 =$

G. $54 \div 6 =$ H. $18 \div 2 =$

I. $81 \div 9 =$ J. $12 \div 3 =$

K. $63 \div 7 =$ L. $21 \div 7 =$

M. $15 \div 5 =$ N. $6 \div 3 =$

O. $27 \div 9 =$ P. $36 \div 4 =$

Q. $72 \div 8 =$

TIMS Bit

A. 10   B. 9
C. 9   D. 3
E. 3   F. 3
G. 9   H. 9
I. 9   J. 4
K. 9   L. 3
M. 3   N. 2
O. 3   P. 9
Q. 9

Student Questions	Teacher Notes

 Practice

Solve the following problems using a paper-and-pencil method. Estimate to be sure your answers are reasonable.

1. A. $18 \times 65 =$

   B. $127 \times 62 =$

   C. $7641 \times 8 =$

2. A. $2309 \div 7 =$

   B. $2459 \div 12 =$

   C. $6608 \div 28 =$

3. Explain your estimation strategies for 1A and 2A.

TIMS Task

Discuss students' estimation strategies.

1. A. 1170
    B. 7874
    C. 61,128

2. A. 329 R6
    B. 204 R11
    C. 236

3. Possible strategies:
    1A. Round 18 up to 20.
    Round 65 down to 60;
    $20 \times 60 = 1200$.

    2A. 2309 is close to 2100.
    $2100 \div 7 = 300$.
    The answer will be more than 300.

 Products of Prime

Solve the following in your head.

   A. $2^2 \times 3^2 =$

   B. $5^2 \times 2^2 =$

   C. $2^3 \times 3 =$

   D. $3^2 \times 7 =$

TIMS Bit

A. 36	B. 100
C. 24	D. 63

Logic

Latisha, Jackie, Edward, and Carlos are planting trees for Arbor Day. Each will plant a different kind of tree. They are planting white pine, red bud, flowering crab, and oak trees. One of them is planting 20 trees while the others are planting 12, 13, and 14 trees. Use the following clues to find who is planting each kind of tree and how many they are planting.

Clues:

A. Latisha will plant more than the girl planting the flowering crab trees and the boy with the oak trees, but she will plant fewer trees than Carlos.

B. Jackie will plant fewer trees than Carlos and the girl planting the red bud trees, but she will plant more than the boy planting the oak trees.

TIMS Challenge

Students should work with a partner or two to complete this challenge. Discuss students' solution strategies. One way to solve the problem is to organize the data in a grid such as the following. The boxes that can be filled in after reading the first clue are shown in the diagram.

	white pine	red bud	flowering crab	oak	20	14	13	12
Latisha		n	n	n	y	n	n	
Jackie	n	n	y	n	n	n		
Edward	n	n	n	y	n	n		
Carlos		n	n	n	y	n	n	n
20		n	n					
14		n	n					
13								
12								

Latisha: 14 red bud trees

Jackie: 13 flowering crab trees

Edward: 12 oak trees

Carlos: 20 white pine trees

Lesson 1

Factor 40

Lesson Overview

Students explore factors while playing the game *Factor 40*. They analyze first moves after charting the factors of the numbers 1 through 40. Students identify prime numbers and composite numbers and use the information to develop strategies for playing *Factor 40*.

Key Content

- Finding all the factors of numbers.
- Identifying prime and composite numbers.

Key Vocabulary

- composite
- factor
- prime

Homework

1. Assign the Homework section in the *Student Guide*.
2. Assign Part 1 of the Home Practice.

Assessment

1. Use homework *Questions 6–8* as an assessment.
2. Use the *Observational Assessment Record* to note students' abilities to find all the factors of a number.

Curriculum Sequence

Before This Unit

Students studied factors, multiples, prime numbers, and composite numbers in Grade 4 Unit 4.

Materials List

Supplies and Copies

Student	Teacher
Supplies for Each Student • calculator	**Supplies**
Copies • 4 copies of *Three-column Data Table* per student, optional (*Unit Resource Guide* Page 32)	**Copies/Transparencies** • 1 copy of *Observational Assessment Record* to be used throughout this unit (*Unit Resource Guide* Pages 11–12) • 1 transparency of *Factor 40 Game Board* (*Discovery Assignment Book* Page 181)

All blackline masters including assessment, transparency, and DPP masters are also on the Teacher Resource CD.

Student Books
Factor 40 (*Student Guide* Pages 348–352)
Factor 40 Game Board (*Discovery Assignment Book* Page 181)

Daily Practice and Problems and Home Practice
DPP items A–D (*Unit Resource Guide* Pages 14–15)
Home Practice Part 1 (*Discovery Assignment Book* Page 177)

Note: Classrooms whose pacing differs significantly from the suggested pacing of the units should use the Math Facts Calendar in Section 4 of the *Facts Resource Guide* to ensure students receive the complete math facts program.

Assessment Tools
Observational Assessment Record (*Unit Resource Guide* Pages 11–12)

Daily Practice and Problems

Suggestions for using the DPPs are on page 30.

A. Bit: Multiplication and Division (URG p. 14)

Solve each problem using paper and pencil.

A. $234 \times 6 =$ B. $24,000 \div 60 =$

C. $26 \times 14 =$ D. $903 \div 7 =$

B. Task: Parent-Teacher Conferences (URG p. 14)

Mr. Moreno plans to meet with the parents of each of his 22 students during Parent-Teacher Conferences. The conferences are held from 4:00 to 6:00 P.M. and from 7:00 to 9:00 P.M. (There is a one hour dinner break for the teachers from 6:00 to 7:00.)

1. About how long can Mr. Moreno meet with the parents of each student, if they all plan to come to the conferences?

2. Mr. Moreno finds out that 2 parents are unable to attend the conferences. Eight parents need to come between 7:00 and 9:00 because of their work schedules. The rest of the parents will come between 4 and 6 o'clock. Help Mr. Moreno schedule his conferences.

C. Bit: Less Than One (URG p. 15)

Without a calculator, decide which of the following products are less than one. Explain your reasoning.

A. $7.32 \times 0.5 =$

B. $2.36 \times 0.04 =$

C. $180.3 \times 0.002 =$

D. Challenge: Coordinated Coordinates (URG p. 15)

Use a sheet of graph paper to help you with this problem. Write down some ordered pairs in which the x-coordinates are equal in value to the y-coordinates. Plot the points and describe the resulting graph. Filling in this table first may help.

x	y
2	2
-2	-2

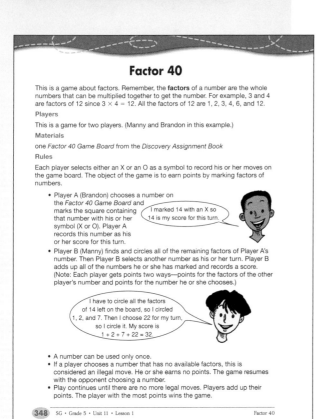

Student Guide - page 348

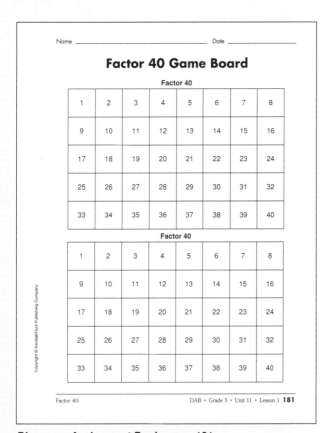

Discovery Assignment Book - page 181

Begin this lesson by reviewing factors with your students. To get started, ask:

- *List the factors of 6 and 24.* (The factors of 6 are 1, 2, 3, and 6. The factors of 24 are 1, 2, 3, 4, 6, 8, 12, and 24.)

- *Write what you know about factors in your journals.*

Possible student responses include:

- Factors of a number are numbers you multiply together to get that number.

- Factors are the numbers you multiply together in a multiplication problem.

- 2 and 3 are factors of 6, because you multiply them together to get 6.

- 3 is a factor of 6 because 3 divides 6 evenly.

Allow time for students to share some of their ideas with the class. Make sure students remember that **factors** are whole numbers that can be multiplied to get a number. That is, the factors of a number are the numbers that divide the number evenly. A number that has exactly two factors—one and itself—is called a **prime number.** If a number has more than 2 different factors it is a **composite number** (it is composed of other numbers). By definition, 1 is not a prime number.

Teaching the Activity

Part 1 *Factor 40*

To introduce this game, show a transparency of the *Factor 40 Game Board* from the *Discovery Assignment Book.* Explain that students will play a factor game with a partner. Read through the rules of the game in the *Factor 40* Game Pages in the *Student Guide.* Using X and O to designate each player's move, mark the game board as if Brandon (Player A) and Manny (Player B) had made the moves suggested in the *Student Guide.* At this point, your game board should look like Figure 1. On Brandon's first turn he marked 14. Manny circled 1, 2, and 7 that are the remaining factors of 14. Then Manny chose 22 for his turn. (Brandon's score is 14 and Manny's is 22 + 7 + 2 + 1 or 32.)

①	②	3	4	5	6	⑦	8
9	10	11	12	13	✗	15	16
17	18	19	20	21	㉒	23	24

Figure 1: *Manny and Brandon's game board*

Next, it would be Brandon's turn to factor Manny's number (22) and then choose another number by marking it with an X. Ask students:

- *What are the factors of 22?* (1, 2, 11, and 22)
- *What number(s) should Brandon mark?* (11 is the only available factor of 22 that is left on the game board.)

Ask your class to suggest a number for Brandon and mark it on the game board with an X. Choose a number for Brandon that would be an illegal move—for example, 37. Ask students why Brandon's choice is illegal. Remind students that if you choose a number with no available factors you lose those points and the points you earned on this turn from factoring. Brandon does not receive the points for the illegal number (37) nor does he receive the points for the factor he marked for Manny's number (11). The game continues with Manny choosing a number for Brandon to factor.

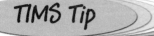

Each pair of students will need one copy of the *Factor 40 Game Board* Game Page from the *Discovery Assignment Book*. Since there are two game boards on each student's page, student pairs are able to play four games. You may want to make additional copies of the boards so students can take them home to play the game with a family member.

Continue the game for one or two more moves if students are still unclear about the instructions. Otherwise, allow them to begin the game. The directions for the game in the *Student Guide* ask students to play the game twice. In Part 2 they will play the game two more times after they develop some strategies for playing.

Journal Prompt

Think about the moves that you and your partner made while playing *Factor 40*. What strategies can help make you more successful at this game?

Part 2 What's the Best First Move?
Ask students to share their strategies *(Question 1)*. Then turn to the *Student Guide* pages and read about Brandon's strategy of creating a factor chart.

Students should begin work on *Questions 2–6* in the *Student Guide*. *Question 2A* asks students to copy Brandon's chart. Students can use copies of the *Three-column Data Table* or they can create three columns

---

Here is what Brandon's and Manny's game board looks like so far. Remember, Brandon is Player A and Manny is Player B.

Play the game twice with a partner.

1. While playing the game a second time, think about the moves you and your partner make. Were you more successful in the second game? Describe any strategies you used or things you learned while playing the second time around.

After Manny and Brandon finished their second game of *Factor 40*, Brandon began thinking about the moves that he made during the game. He realized that sometimes when he chose a number to mark, Manny actually got more points on his next turn. This was because the sum of the factors was sometimes greater than the number chosen. For example, in the second game Brandon marked 24 for his first move. Manny was then able to circle 1, 2, 3, 4, 6, 8, and 12. Brandon only got 24 points, while Manny scored 36 before he chose his own number!

①	②	③	④	5	⑥	7	⑧
9	10	11	⑫	13	14	15	16
17	18	19	20	21	22	23	⨯

Factor 40   SG • Grade 5 • Unit 11 • Lesson 1   **349**

Student Guide - page 349 (Answers on p. 33)

Brandon decided to make a chart showing all of the factors for the numbers 1 through 40. He wanted to use the chart to find the best first move for the game.

Factor Chart

Possible First Choice for Player A	Factors	Points from Factors for Player B (first move)
1	1	0
2	1, 2	1
3	1, 3	1
4	1, 2, 4	1 + 2 = 3
5	1, 5	1
6	1, 2, 3, 6	1 + 2 + 3 = 6
7	1, 7	
8		

Explore

2. A. Copy Brandon's chart on your paper. Fill in the first column with the numbers 1 to 40.
   B. Complete the second column of the chart for all the numbers from 1 to 40. Be prepared to describe the strategies you used.
   C. Complete the third column of the chart. Find how many points Player B will get for each number Player A might choose on the first move.

3. A. Look at your chart. Make a list of all the first moves that give Player A more points than Player B. (Remember, Player B's score will also be determined by the number he or she chooses. We are comparing Player A's points with Player B's points *before* Player B chooses his or her number.)
   B. Make a list of all of the moves that will give Player B more points than Player A (if Player B marks all of the factors of Player A's number left on the board).

350   SG • Grade 5 • Unit 11 • Lesson 1   Factor 40

Student Guide - page 350 (Answers on p. 33)

on lined paper. (Note: Students need rows for the numbers 1 to 40.) Assign **Question 2B** as homework after playing *Factor 40* several times or complete it in class. However, before beginning **Question 2B,** you will need to discuss strategies students can use to find all the factors.

The following prompts outline a strategy for finding all the factors of 32. Encourage students to use calculators.

- *Is 1 a factor of 32? How do you know?* (Yes. Since $1 \times 32 = 32$, 1 and 32 are both factors of 32. Write 1 and 32 in the second column of your chart in the row for 32.)
- *Is 2 a factor of 32?* (Yes. $2 \times 16 = 32$. Record 2 and 16 in your chart.)
- *Is 3 a factor of 32?* (No. Since $32 \div 3 = 10$ R2 or 10.666667 on your calculator, 3 is not a factor of 32.)

- *Is 4 a factor of 32?* (Yes. $4 \times 8 = 32$. Record 4 and 8 in your chart.)
- *Is 5 a factor of 32?* (No.)
- *Is 6 a factor of 32?* (No.)
- *Is 7 a factor of 32?* (No.)
- *Is 8 a factor of 32?* (Yes. We already wrote it down. Since we are now repeating factors, we know we have found all possible factors.)

Students may also realize that while an even number can have both odd and even factors, an odd number has only odd factors. Therefore, another strategy they can use when finding factors of an odd number is to check only odd numbers for their factor pairs. Once students complete **Question 2B,** you may want to compile the information on a class chart as in Figure 2.

Possible First Choice for Player A	Factors	Points from Factors for Player B (first move)	Possible First Choice for Player A	Factors	Points from Factors for Player B (first move)
1	1	0	21	1, 3, 7, 21	11
2	1, 2	1	22	1, 2, 11, 22	14
3	1, 3	1	23	1, 23	1
4	1, 2, 4	3	24	1, 2, 3, 4, 6, 8, 12, 24	36
5	1, 5	1	25	1, 5, 25	6
6	1, 2, 3, 6	6	26	1, 2, 13, 26	16
7	1, 7	1	27	1, 3, 9, 27	13
8	1, 2, 4, 8	7	28	1, 2, 4, 7, 14, 28	28
9	1, 3, 9	4	29	1, 29	1
10	1, 2, 5, 10	8	30	1, 2, 3, 5, 6, 10, 15, 30	42
11	1, 11	1	31	1, 31	1
12	1, 2, 3, 4, 6, 12	16	32	1, 2, 4, 8, 16, 32	31
13	1, 13	1	33	1, 3, 11, 33	15
14	1, 2, 7, 14	10	34	1, 2, 17, 34	20
15	1, 3, 5, 15	9	35	1, 5, 7, 35	13
16	1, 2, 4, 8, 16	15	36	1, 2, 3, 4, 6, 9, 12, 18, 36	55
17	1, 17	1	37	1, 37	1
18	1, 2, 3, 6, 9, 18	21	38	1, 2, 19, 38	22
19	1, 19	1	39	1, 3, 13, 39	17
20	1, 2, 4, 5, 10, 20	22	40	1, 2, 4, 5, 8, 10, 20, 40	50

Figure 2: *Factor chart for first moves in* Factor 40

Question 2C asks students to complete the third column, Points from Factors for Player B. Remind students the numbers in the first column designate the number Player A marks on the first move. Player A receives the points for the number itself. Player B, on his or her first turn, receives points for all the other factors. Students should add up the factors of each number in each row excluding the number itself. See Figure 2.

TIMS Tip

When computing the points for Player B (see the third column in Figure 2), remind students *not* to include the number itself when adding the factors of a number. For example, look at the row for 18 in Figure 2. The factors of 18 are 1, 2, 3, 6, 9, and 18. Since Player A chooses the number 18, he or she receives 18 points. Player B's score is the sum of the remaining factors— 1 + 2 + 3 + 6 + 9 or 21 points.

In *Question 3,* students analyze their charts to find the moves that would give Player A more points than Player B, fewer points than Player B, or the same number of points as Player B. (Note: Player B will also earn points on his or her turn for the number he or she chooses. In analyzing first moves, however, we are concentrating only on the points Player B receives from the factors of the number chosen by Player A.) For example, Player A receives more points for choosing 14 than Player B who receives only 10 points (1 + 2 + 7). However, Player A receives fewer points for choosing 18 than Player B who receives 21 points.

After completing *Questions 4–5,* students conclude that all prime numbers become illegal moves after Player B's first move. This is because a prime number has exactly two distinct factors, 1 and itself. Since one is a factor of every number, it should be marked by Player B after the first number is chosen by Player A. Therefore, prime numbers have no unmarked factors after Player B's first move. The prime numbers from 1 to 40 are: 2, 3, 5, 7, 11, 13, 17, 19, 23, 29, 31, and 37.

After students complete *Questions 1–6,* they should play *Factor 40* two more times using information they learned.

Content Note

One Is Not Prime. Since a prime number is defined as a number with exactly two factors, one is not considered to be prime.

C. Make a list of all of the moves that will give Player A the same number of points as Player B (if he marks them all).

4. A. No matter which number Player A chooses on his or her first move, which factor will Player B definitely mark on his or her first turn?
   B. It is illegal to mark a number that does not have any available factors. After Player B's first turn, which numbers are illegal moves?

5. A **prime number** is defined as a number with exactly two factors—1 and itself. Make a list of all the prime numbers from 1 to 40. Compare this list with the list you made in Question 4B. What do you notice about the two lists?

6. A **composite number** is a number with more than 2 distinct (or different) factors. Which are the composite numbers on your chart?

   Since the number 1 doesn't have 2 distinct factors, it is not considered prime or composite.

7. Use your lists and what you have learned as you play another game of *Factor 40*. See if your lists help you as you choose your moves.

Complete the following questions. You can use a calculator to help you find factors.

1. Irma and Jackie are playing *Factor 40* in class. Jackie is the first player. She chooses 27 as her first number.
   A. What are the factors of 27 that Irma can mark?
   B. How many points will Irma earn for these factors?

2. Felicia and Jessie designed a *Factor 100* game board. *Factor 100* has the same rules as *Factor 40*. It includes the numbers 1 to 100. Felicia is the first player. She chooses 40 as her first number.
   A. What are the factors of 40 that Jessie can mark?
   B. How many points will Jessie earn for these factors?

3. Romesh and David are playing *Factor 100*. David is the first player. He chooses 76 as his first move.
   A. What factors of 76 can Romesh mark?
   B. How many points will Romesh earn for these factors?

Factor 40   SG • Grade 5 • Unit 11 • Lesson 1   **351**

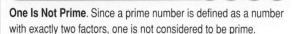

Student Guide - page 351 (Answers on p. 34)

Student Guide page (boxed)

4. Nicholas and Michael are playing *Factor 100*. Nicholas is the first player. He wants to choose either 84 or 92 as his first move.
   A. Find the factors of both 84 and 92.
   B. Which number is a better move for Nicholas?
   C. Explain your answer.

5. Edward and Nila are playing *Factor 100*. Nila is the first player. She chooses 72 as her first move. Edward marks 1, 2, 3, 8, 9, and 24. He recorded 47 points.
   A. Did Edward mark all the possible factors of 72? If not, what other numbers could he mark?
   B. If Edward marks all the factors he can, how many points will he earn?

6. List all the factors of the following numbers.
   A. 31
   B. 56
   C. 63
   D. 67
   E. 100

7. Which of the numbers in Question 6 are prime? How do you know?

8. Which of the numbers in Question 6 are composite? How do you know?

Student Guide - page 352 (Answers on p. 34)

Discovery Assignment Book page (boxed)

Name _____ Date _____

Unit 11 Home Practice

PART 1 Multiplication and Division Practice
Use paper and pencil to solve the following problems. Estimate to be sure your answers are reasonable.

1. A. 2170 ÷ 52 =   B. 28 × 69 =
   C. 1307 × 9 =   D. 9603 ÷ 3 =

2. Explain your estimation strategies for Questions 1A and 1C.

PART 2 Going to the Theater
Arti and Lin helped collect tickets at Arti's mother's theater. Tickets for the play are $14 for adults and $9 for students. Adult theater members get a discount and only have to pay half-price ($7).

Number of Tickets in Each Category

Performance	Adult Tickets (full price)	Student Tickets	Adult Member Tickets
Friday	97	15	13
Saturday	103	21	20
Sunday	82	43	5

1. How many people attended each performance of the play?

2. Find the amount of money collected for each performance.

3. How many more adults than students saw the play?

Copyright © Kendall/Hunt Publishing Company

NUMBER PATTERNS, PRIMES, AND FRACTIONS   DAB • Grade 5 • Unit 11 **177**

Discovery Assignment Book - page 177 (Answers on p. 35)

Homework and Practice

- Assign **Questions 2B–2C** on the *Factor 40* Game Pages in the *Student Guide* as homework after students play *Factor 40* in class.

- Students can play this game at home with a family member. Send home the *Student Guide* directions and a copy of the *Factor 40 Game Board* Game Page from the *Discovery Assignment Book*.

- Assign DPP items A–C. Bit A practices multiplication and division computation. Task B involves problem solving with time. Bit C involves estimating products with decimals.

- Assign the Homework section in the *Student Guide* after Part 2 of this lesson.

- Assign Part 1 of the Home Practice that reviews multiplication and division computation.

Answers for Part 1 of the Home Practice are in the Answer Key at the end of this lesson and at the end of this unit.

Assessment

- Use Homework **Questions 6–8** in the *Student Guide* as an assessment.

- Use the *Observational Assessment Record* to note students' abilities to find all the factors of a number.

Extension

- Design *Factor 100*. Analyze first moves.

- Play *Factor 40* cooperatively with a partner. Try to get the most points.

- DPP item D provides a challenging question using ordered pairs.

At a Glance

Math Facts and Daily Practice and Problems

Assign DPP items A–D that involve computation, time, number sense, and coordinate geometry.

Before the Activity

1. Students review factors by listing the factors of several numbers.
2. Students write what they know about factors in their math journals. They share these ideas with the class. Review the terms prime and composite numbers.

Part 1. Factor 40

1. Introduce the game *Factor 40*, using an overhead transparency of the *Factor 40 Game Board* Game Page in the *Discovery Assignment Book*. Play a game with the class to introduce the rules that are in the *Factor 40* Game Pages in the *Student Guide*.
2. Students play two games of *Factor 40* with a partner.
3. Students complete the Journal Prompt.

Part 2. What's the Best First Move?

1. Students share their strategies. *(Question 1)*
2. Read about Brandon's factor chart in the *Student Guide*.
3. Students copy Brandon's chart. *(Question 2A)* After discussing strategies for finding the factors of a number, students complete *Question 2B*.
4. Students complete *Questions 2–6*. Discuss answers in class.
5. Students play *Factor 40* again using what they learned by completing the factor chart. *(Question 7)*

Homework

1. Assign the Homework section in the *Student Guide*.
2. Assign Part 1 of the Home Practice.

Assessment

1. Use homework *Questions 6–8* as an assessment.
2. As students play *Factor 40*, note their abilities to find all the factors of a number on the *Observational Assessment Record*.

Extension

1. Design *Factor 100*. Analyze first moves.
2. Play *Factor 40* cooperatively with a partner. Try to get the most points.
3. Assign DPP item D.

Answer Key is on pages 33–35.

Notes:

Name _____ Date _____

_____

Three-column Data Table, Blackline Master

Student Guide (p. 349)

1. Answers will vary. See discussion in Part 2 of Lesson Guide 1.*

Here is what Brandon's and Manny's game board looks like so far. Remember, Brandon is Player A and Manny is Player B.

Play the game twice with a partner.

1. While playing the game a second time, think about the moves you and your partner make. Were you more successful in the second game? Describe any strategies you used or things you learned while playing the second time around.

After Manny and Brandon finished their second game of *Factor 40*, Brandon began thinking about the moves that he made during the game. He realized that sometimes when he chose a number to mark, Manny actually got more points on his next turn. This was because the sum of the factors was sometimes greater than the number chosen. For example, in the second game Brandon marked 24 for his first move. Manny was then able to circle 1, 2, 3, 4, 6, 8, and 12. Brandon only got 24 points, while Manny scored 36 before he chose his own number!

1	2	3	4	5	6	7	8
9	10	11	12	13	14	15	16
17	18	19	20	21	22	23	24

Factor 40   SG • Grade 5 • Unit 11 • Lesson 1   **349**

Student Guide - page 349

Student Guide (p. 350)

2. See Figure 2 in Lesson Guide 1.*

3.* **A.** Player A gets more points than Player B when Player A's first choice is: 2, 3, 4, 5, 7, 8, 9, 10, 11, 13, 14, 15, 16, 17, 19, 21, 22, 23, 25, 26, 27, 29, 31, 32, 33, 34, 35, 37, 38, or 39.

  B. Player B gets more points than Player A when Player A's first choice is: 12, 18, 20, 24, 30, 36, or 40.

Brandon decided to make a chart showing all of the factors for the numbers 1 through 40. He wanted to use the chart to find the best first move for the game.

Factor Chart

Possible First Choice for Player A	Factors	Points from Factors for Player B (first move)
1	1	0
2	1, 2	1
3	1, 3	1
4	1, 2, 4	1 + 2 = 3
5	1, 5	1
6	1, 2, 3, 6	1 + 2 + 3 = 6
7	1, 7	
8		

2. **A.** Copy Brandon's chart on your paper. Fill in the first column with the numbers 1 to 40.
   B. Complete the second column of the chart for all the numbers from 1 to 40. Be prepared to describe the strategies you used.
   C. Complete the third column of the chart. Find how many points Player B will get for each number Player A might choose on the first move.

3. **A.** Look at your chart. Make a list of all the first moves that give Player A more points than Player B. (Remember, Player B's score will also be determined by the number he or she chooses. We are comparing Player A's points with Player B's points *before* Player B chooses his or her number.)
   B. Make a list of all of the moves that will give Player B more points than Player A (if Player B marks all of the factors of Player A's number left on the board).

350   SG • Grade 5 • Unit 11 • Lesson 1   Factor 40

Student Guide - page 350

*Answers and/or discussion are included in the Lesson Guide.

C. Make a list of all of the moves that will give Player A the same number of points as Player B (if he marks them all).

4. A. No matter which number Player A chooses on his or her first move, which factor will Player B definitely mark on his or her first turn?
   B. It is illegal to mark a number that does not have any available factors. After Player B's first turn, which numbers are illegal moves?

5. A **prime number** is defined as a number with exactly two factors—1 and itself. Make a list of all of the prime numbers from 1 to 40. Compare this list with the list you made in Question 4B. What do you notice about the two lists?

6. A **composite number** is a number with more than 2 distinct (or different) factors. Which are the composite numbers on your chart?

> Since the number 1 doesn't have 2 distinct factors, it is not considered prime or composite.

7. Use your lists and what you have learned as you play another game of *Factor 40.* See if your lists help you as you choose your moves.

Homework

Complete the following questions. You can use a calculator to help you find factors.

1. Irma and Jackie are playing *Factor 40* in class. Jackie is the first player. She chooses 27 as her first number.
   A. What are the factors of 27 that Irma can mark?
   B. How many points will Irma earn for these factors?

2. Felicia and Jessie designed a *Factor 100* game board. *Factor 100* has the same rules as *Factor 40.* It includes the numbers 1 to 100. Felicia is the first player. She chooses 40 as her first number.
   A. What are the factors of 40 that Jessie can mark?
   B. How many points will Jessie earn for these factors?

3. Romesh and David are playing *Factor 100.* David is the first player. He chooses 76 as his first move.
   A. What factors of 76 can Romesh mark?
   B. How many points will Romesh earn for these factors?

Factor 40 SG • Grade 5 • Unit 11 • Lesson 1 351

***Student Guide* - page 351**

4. Nicholas and Michael are playing *Factor 100.* Nicholas is the first player. He wants to choose either 84 or 92 as his first move.
   A. Find the factors of both 84 and 92.
   B. Which number is a better move for Nicholas?
   C. Explain your answer.

5. Edward and Nila are playing *Factor 100.* Nila is the first player. She chooses 72 as her first move. Edward marks 1, 2, 3, 8, 9, and 24. He recorded 47 points.
   A. Did Edward mark all the possible factors of 72? If not, what other numbers could he mark?
   B. If Edward marks all the factors he can, how many points will he earn?

6. List all the factors of the following numbers.
   A. 31
   B. 56
   C. 63
   D. 67
   E. 100

7. Which of the numbers in Question 6 are prime? How do you know?

8. Which of the numbers in Question 6 are composite? How do you know?

352 SG • Grade 5 • Unit 11 • Lesson 1 Factor 40

***Student Guide* - page 352**

*Answers and/or discussion are included in the Lesson Guide.

Student Guide (pp. 351–352)

C. Player A gets the same points as Player B when Player A's first choice is: 6 or 28.

4. A. 1
   B. The numbers that have exactly two factors—1 and itself (i.e., the prime numbers). 1 is illegal on the first move.*

5. 2, 3, 5, 7, 11, 13, 17, 19, 23, 29, 31, 37*

6. 4, 6, 8, 9, 10, 12, 14, 15, 16, 18, 20, 21, 22, 24, 25, 26, 27, 28, 30, 32, 33, 34, 35, 36, 38, 39, 40

7. Students play the game. Their lists should help them choose their moves.

Homework

1. A. 1, 3, and 9
   B. 13 points

2. A. 1, 2, 4, 5, 8, 10, and 20
   B. 50 points

3. A. 1, 2, 4, 19, and 38
   B. 64 points

4. A. Factors of 84: 1, 2, 3, 4, 6, 7, 12, 14, 21, 28, 42, 84
   Factors of 92: 1, 2, 4, 23, 46, 92
   B. 92
   C. If Nicholas chooses 84, Michael gets 140 points, more points than Nicholas gets. But if Nicholas chooses 92, then Michael only gets 76 points. Therefore, 92 is a better choice than 84 for Nicholas.

5. A. No. Edward should also mark 4, 6, 12, 18, and 36.
   B. 123 points

6. A. 1 and 31
   B. 1, 2, 4, 7, 8, 14, 28, and 56
   C. 1, 7, 9, and 63
   D. 1 and 67
   E. 1, 2, 4, 5, 10, 20, 25, 50, and 100

7. 31 and 67 are prime numbers because their only factors are 1 and themselves.

8. 56, 63, and 100 are composite numbers because they have more than two factors.

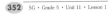

Discovery Assignment Book (p. 177)

Home Practice*

Part 1. Multiplication and Division Practice

I. **A.** 41 R38

  B. 1932

  C. 11, 763

  D. 3201

2. Strategies will vary. One possible strategy is given for each.

For 1A: $2000 \div 50 = 40$

For 1C: Between

$1000 \times 9 = 9000$ and

$1300 \times 10 = 13{,}000$

Name _____ Date _____

Unit 11 **Home Practice**

PART 1 **Multiplication and Division Practice**

Use paper and pencil to solve the following problems. Estimate to be sure your answers are reasonable.

1. **A.** $2170 \div 52 =$ **B.** $28 \times 69 =$

  C. $1307 \times 9 =$ **D.** $9603 \div 3 =$

2. Explain your estimation strategies for Questions 1A and 1C.

PART 2 **Going to the Theater**

Arti and Lin helped collect tickets at Arti's mother's theater. Tickets for the play are $14 for adults and $9 for students. Adult theater members get a discount and only have to pay half-price ($7).

Number of Tickets in Each Category

Performance	Adult Tickets (full price)	Student Tickets	Adult Member Tickets
Friday	97	15	13
Saturday	103	21	20
Sunday	82	43	5

1. How many people attended each performance of the play?

2. Find the amount of money collected for each performance.

3. How many more adults than students saw the play?

NUMBER PATTERNS, PRIMES, AND FRACTIONS   DAB • Grade 5 • Unit 11 **177**

Discovery Assignment Book - page 177

---

*Answers for all the Home Practice in the *Discovery Assignment Book* are at the end of the unit.

Lesson 2

Sifting for Primes

Lesson Overview

Estimated Class Sessions

1

Students identify the prime numbers between 1 and 200 using the Sieve of Eratosthenes. Students look for patterns that develop on the 200 chart as primes are identified.

Key Content

- Identifying prime numbers.
- Identifying and describing number patterns.

Key Vocabulary

- conjecture
- cryptography
- Eratosthenes
- sieve
- twin primes

Math Facts

DPP Bit E reviews the division facts for the 3s and 9s.

Homework

1. Students sift for the prime numbers from 101 to 200 on the *200 Chart* Activity Page in the *Discovery Assignment Book.*
2. Assign Part 2 of the Home Practice.

Assessment

Use the *Observational Assessment Record* to note students' abilities to identify prime numbers.

Curriculum Sequence

Before This Unit

Students investigated prime and composite numbers in Grade 4 Unit 4. In Unit 7 of fourth grade, they discussed divisibility rules.

Materials List

Supplies and Copies

Student	Teacher
Supplies for Each Student	**Supplies**
Copies	**Copies/Transparencies** • 1–4 transparencies of *200 Chart*, optional *(Discovery Assignment Book* Page 183)

All blackline masters including assessment, transparency, and DPP masters are also on the Teacher Resource CD.

Student Books
Sifting for Primes (*Student Guide* Pages 353–355)
200 Chart (*Discovery Assignment Book* Page 183)

Daily Practice and Problems and Home Practice
DPP items E–F (*Unit Resource Guide* Pages 15–16)
Home Practice Part 2 (*Discovery Assignment Book* Page 177)

Note: Classrooms whose pacing differs significantly from the suggested pacing of the units should use the Math Facts Calendar in Section 4 of the *Facts Resource Guide* to ensure students receive the complete math facts program.

Assessment Tools
Observational Assessment Record (*Unit Resource Guide* Pages 11–12)

Daily Practice and Problems

Suggestions for using the DPPs are on page 41.

E. Bit: Division Practice I (URG p. 15)

A. $72 \div 9 =$ B. $24 \div 3 =$
C. $45 \div 9 =$ D. $15 \div 3 =$
E. $36 \div 9 =$ F. $12 \div 3 =$

F. Task: Hawaii for Half (URG p. 16)

A travel agent offers Maria a 50% discount on a trip to Hawaii. The trip includes airfare and 11 nights in a hotel. The price for the trip before the discount is $3038. If the airfare will cost Maria $650, what is the cost of the hotel per night after the discount?

TIMS Tip

Bring a colander or strainer from home to show students an example of a sieve.

Teaching the Activity

Read the vignette on the *Sifting for Primes* Activity Pages in the *Student Guide* in small groups or as a class. If necessary, define **sieve.** Students may be more familiar with a colander, a type of sieve used in the kitchen to separate liquids from solids. Just as a colander is used to separate water from something like pasta, the Sieve of Eratosthenes is used to separate prime numbers from nonprime numbers.

Content Note

After reading the vignette in the *Student Guide,* you may want to give students some additional information about prime numbers:

- No one has proved or disproved Goldbach's **Conjecture,** that every even number can be written as the sum of two prime numbers. However, in 1993 a computer did verify that the conjecture is true for every even number up to 100 million.

- There are infinitely many prime numbers. Prime numbers occur less frequently among large numbers. For example, there are 168 prime numbers between 1 and 1000. There are only 75 primes between 1,000,000 and 1,001,000. Both of these intervals include 1000 numbers, but there are more primes in the interval 1 to 1000.

"This book says that Eratosthenes had etched a list of consecutive numbers on a table made on a metal plate. He considered each number one by one and marked each of its multiples with a small hole. The numbers that were not marked in this way were the prime numbers. In the end, it resembled a sieve. Since it was used to separate prime numbers from nonprime numbers, it got the name **The Sieve of Eratosthenes.** He presented this table to a king in Egypt."

Nila added to the discussion. "I found out that in the mid-1800s, an astronomer named J.P. Kulik used the Sieve of Eratosthenes to find the prime numbers up to 100,000,000. He spent 20 years of his life doing this."

"I can't believe anyone would spend 20 years finding prime numbers!" exclaimed Michael.

"The sad part is that Kulik gave his manuscript to a library in Prague. They lost the sections that had the prime numbers from 12,642,000 to 22,852,800," added Mr. Moreno.

"I also found some interesting data," said John. "I found out that in 1742 a Russian mathematician named Christian Goldbach made a conjecture that every even number except 2 can be written as a sum of two prime numbers. For example, $10 = 3 + 7$."

"Right," said Mr. Moreno, "and it is called a **conjecture** because up to now no one has been able to prove or disprove it. Who knows, maybe someday one of you will be the person to do this!"

"I found a modern use for prime numbers," said Lin. "Prime numbers are used in cryptography. **Cryptography** is the study of secret codes. Some codes are based on factoring numbers with 100 or more digits into prime factors. One use of these codes is to protect information stored on computers. Many banks and other businesses use these codes to make sure that nobody can change or steal the information from their computers."

"Wow," said Michael, "with all of this information we should be able to write a great report for class. Let's get started."

354   SG • Grade 5 • Unit 11 • Lesson 2   Sifting for Primes

Student Guide - page 354

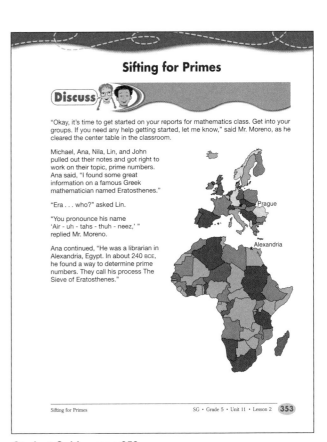

Sifting for Primes

Discuss

"Okay, it's time to get started on your reports for mathematics class. Get into your groups. If you need any help getting started, let me know," said Mr. Moreno, as he cleared the center table in the classroom.

Michael, Ana, Nila, Lin, and John pulled out their notes and got right to work on their topic, prime numbers. Ana said, "I found some great information on a famous Greek mathematician named Eratosthenes."

"Era . . . who?" asked Lin.

"You pronounce his name 'Air - uh - tahs - thuh - neez,' " replied Mr. Moreno.

Ana continued, "He was a librarian in Alexandria, Egypt. In about 240 BCE, he found a way to determine prime numbers. They call his process The Sieve of Eratosthenes."

Prague

Alexandria

Sifting for Primes   SG • Grade 5 • Unit 11 • Lesson 2   353

Student Guide - page 353

After reading and discussing the information in the *Student Guide,* students may begin sifting for the prime numbers between 1 and 100 on the *200 Chart* Activity Page in the *Discovery Assignment Book.* Ask students to fold their charts so they see only the numbers 1 to 100. They should follow the directions in **Questions 1–4** in the *Student Guide.* Students will complete their work on the *200 Chart* Activity Page as they sift for the prime numbers between 101 and 200 for homework.

TIMS Tip

If students are having trouble identifying multiples, review the strategy of skip counting with students. For example, when crossing out the multiples of 2, students can skip count by 2; when crossing out the multiples of 3, students can skip count by 3.

Using a transparency of the *200 Chart* Activity Page, model filling in the chart for the first few numbers as students work at their seats. This will help ensure that each student completes his or her chart correctly.

Allow students to work until they convince themselves that the only numbers left are prime numbers. This may mean that some students will need to continue looking for the multiples of each number on the chart that has not been crossed out (see Figure 3) or they may discover they only have to cross out the multiples of prime numbers.

Figure 3: *Sifting for primes on a 100 chart*

---

200 Chart

1	2	3	4	5	6	7	8	9	10
11	12	13	14	15	16	17	18	19	20
21	22	23	24	25	26	27	28	29	30
31	32	33	34	35	36	37	38	39	40
41	42	43	44	45	46	47	48	49	50
51	52	53	54	55	56	57	58	59	60
61	62	63	64	65	66	67	68	69	70
71	72	73	74	75	76	77	78	79	80
81	82	83	84	85	86	87	88	89	90
91	92	93	94	95	96	97	98	99	100
101	102	103	104	105	106	107	108	109	110
111	112	113	114	115	116	117	118	119	120
121	122	123	124	125	126	127	128	129	130
131	132	133	134	135	136	137	138	139	140
141	142	143	144	145	146	147	148	149	150
151	152	153	154	155	156	157	158	159	160
161	162	163	164	165	166	167	168	169	170
171	172	173	174	175	176	177	178	179	180
181	182	183	184	185	186	187	188	189	190
191	192	193	194	195	196	197	198	199	200

Sifting for Primes   DAB • Grade 5 • Unit 11 • Lesson 2   **183**

Discovery Assignment Book - page 183

TIMS Tip

Instead of using one overhead, prepare four overheads ahead of time. On the first one, circle 2 and cross out all the multiples of 2. On the second transparency, circle 3 and cross out all the multiples of 3. On the third transparency, circle 5 and cross out all the multiples of 5. Complete the fourth transparency by circling 7 and crossing out the multiples of 7. After students complete their sieves through 100, show them a completed sieve by using the transparencies as overlays, one at a time.

You can use the Sieve of Eratosthenes to find all of the prime numbers between 1 and 100. Use the *200 Chart* Activity Page in the *Discovery Assignment Book*.

1. Begin by crossing out the number 1. (Remember, 1 is not a prime.)

2. **A.** The next number is 2. This is the first prime number. Circle the number 2. Cross out all of the multiples of 2 up to 100.
   B. Why can't any of the numbers you crossed out be prime?

3. **A.** Find the next number that is not circled or crossed out. What number is it?
   B. Is this a prime number?
   C. Circle this number. Cross out all of the multiples of this number up to 100.
   D. Why can't these numbers be prime?

4. Continue the steps in Question 3 until you have only prime numbers left on your chart. List all the prime numbers from 1 to 100.

5. **A.** As you made your chart, what patterns did you see?
   B. What digits do prime numbers end in?
   C. Are prime numbers ever next to each other?
   D. **Twin primes** are pairs of prime numbers that are separated by only one number. For example, 5 and 7 are twin primes. Can you find any other twin primes?

Homework

Continue your investigation of prime numbers by finding all the prime numbers between 1 and 200.

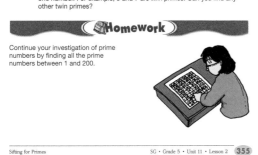

Sifting for Primes SG • Grade 5 • Unit 11 • Lesson 2 **355**

***Student Guide* - page 355** *(Answers on p. 43)*

Content Note

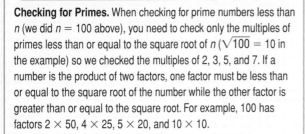

Checking for Primes. When checking for prime numbers less than *n* (we did *n* = 100 above), you need to check only the multiples of primes less than or equal to the square root of *n* ($\sqrt{100} = 10$ in the example) so we checked the multiples of 2, 3, 5, and 7. If a number is the product of two factors, one factor must be less than or equal to the square root of the number while the other factor is greater than or equal to the square root. For example, 100 has factors 2×50, 4×25, 5×20, and 10×10.

Ask students:

• *When were you sure that all the remaining numbers in the chart were primes and not composite numbers that you had not yet crossed out?*

To help them think about this, offer the following facts.

• When students crossed out the multiples of 2, they eliminated every even number up to 100 from the chart (except for 2), since every even number is a multiple of 2.

• When they cross out the multiples of 3, they only need to cross out 3 times an odd factor since 3 times an even number will equal an even number that was already crossed out. Therefore, students will cross out the following multiples: $3 \times 3 = 9$, $3 \times 5 = 15$, $3 \times 7 = 21$, and so on.

• When crossing out multiples of 5, students will cross out those multiples of 5 that are not multiples of 2 or 3 (since multiples of 2 and 3 were already eliminated).

• To cross out the multiples of 7, students will cross out all multiples of 7 that are not multiples of 2, 3, or 5.

Students will realize that they need not find multiples of any prime number over 50. This is because all multiples of numbers over 50 will be larger than 100. In fact, when finding prime numbers less than 100, they need only check for multiples of the prime numbers 2, 3, 5, and 7. The next prime is 11. The first multiple of 11 that was not already crossed out because it is not a multiple of a smaller prime number is 11×11. But since 11×11 is greater than 100, you do not need to cross out multiples of 11. All the remaining numbers are prime.

Question 4 asks students to list all the primes between 1 and 100—all the numbers that are not crossed out. After students complete their charts to 100, give them time to look for patterns ***(Question 5)***. Students can work in small groups for this part of the lesson. They can write their observations in their journals or on note cards. Share their observations. Responses might include:

• You only need to find the multiples of prime numbers.

• 2 is the only even prime number.

• Except for 2 and 5, prime numbers don't end in 2, 4, 5, 6, 8, or 0.

- Prime numbers do end in 1, 3, 7, and 9. However, not all numbers that end in 1, 3, 7, or 9 are primes.

- Some prime numbers are only separated by one other number like 3 and 5, 11 and 13, or 17 and 19.

   (These are called **twin primes.**)

- 2 and 3 are the only two primes that are next to each other.

Once students have sifted for primes from 1 to 100, assign the Homework section that asks them to find the primes from 101 to 200. Students should work on the same chart that was started in class (the *200 Chart* Activity Page in the *Discovery Assignment Book*). Remind students that they will have to begin by crossing out all of the multiples of 2 from 101–200. They will then cross out the multiples of 3, the multiples of 5, and so on. After they complete the assignment, discuss that they only needed to check up to multiples of 13.

Math Facts

DPP item E practices the division facts for the 3s and the 9s.

Homework and Practice

- Students sift for the prime numbers from 101 to 200 on the *200 Chart* Activity Page in the *Discovery Assignment Book.*

- Assign DPP Task F which involves solving a problem using percent, money, and computation.

- Assign Part 2 of the Home Practice that provides practice with reading and interpreting data in a table.

Answers for Part 2 of the Home Practice are in the Answer Key at the end of this lesson and at the end of this unit.

Assessment

Use the *Observational Assessment Record* to note students' abilities to identify prime numbers.

Content Note

The value of the largest prime known as of 2001 is $2^{13466917} - 1$, which, if written out, would contain 4,053,946 digits.

Name _____ Date _____

Unit 11 Home Practice

PART 1 Multiplication and Division Practice
Use paper and pencil to solve the following problems. Estimate to be sure your answers are reasonable.

1. A. $2170 \div 52 =$ B. $28 \times 69 =$

   C. $1307 \times 9 =$ D. $9603 \div 3 =$

2. Explain your estimation strategies for Questions 1A and 1C.

PART 2 Going to the Theater
Arti and Lin helped collect tickets at Arti's mother's theater. Tickets for the play are $14 for adults and $9 for students. Adult theater members get a discount and only have to pay half-price ($7).

Number of Tickets in Each Category

Performance	Adult Tickets (full price)	Student Tickets	Adult Member Tickets
Friday	97	15	13
Saturday	103	21	20
Sunday	82	43	5

1. How many people attended each performance of the play?

2. Find the amount of money collected for each performance.

3. How many more adults than students saw the play?

NUMBER PATTERNS, PRIMES, AND FRACTIONS   DAB • Grade 5 • Unit 11 **177**

Discovery Assignment Book - page 177 (Answers on p. 43)

At a Glance

Math Facts and Daily Practice and Problems

DPP Bit E reviews the division facts for the 3s and 9s. Task F is a problem with percent and money.

Teaching the Activity

1. Read the vignette on the *Sifting for Primes* Activity Pages in the *Student Guide.* Clarify the meaning of sieve if needed.
2. Students fold back the *200 Chart* Activity Page in the *Discovery Assignment Book* so only the numbers 1 to 100 show. (The remaining numbers will be used for homework.)
3. Students sift for the prime numbers from 1 to 100 using *Questions 1–4* in the *Student Guide.*
4. Students use their charts to list all the primes less than 100. *(Question 4)*
5. Students work in small groups to identify patterns in the chart. *(Question 5)*
6. Discuss how the Sieve of Eratosthenes works.

Homework

1. Students sift for the prime numbers from 101 to 200 on the *200 Chart* Activity Page in the *Discovery Assignment Book.*
2. Assign Part 2 of the Home Practice.

Assessment

Use the *Observational Assessment Record* to note students' abilities to identify prime numbers.

Answer Key is on page 43.

Notes:

Student Guide (p. 355)

2. **B.** They cannot be prime because they have at least one more factor, 2, other than 1 and the number itself.

3. **A.** 3

   B. Yes, the factors of 3 are only 1 and 3.

   D. They cannot be prime because they have at least one more factor, 3, other than 1 and the number itself.

4. See Figure 3 in Lesson Guide 2. 2, 3, 5, 7, 11, 13, 17, 19, 23, 29, 31, 37, 41, 43, 47, 53, 59, 61, 67, 71, 73, 79, 83, 89, and 97*

5. **A.** Answers will vary.*

   B. 1, 3, 7, and 9

   C. Yes, 2 and 3 are next to each other.

   D. 11 and 13, 17 and 19, 29 and 31, 41 and 43, 59 and 61, and 71 and 73

Homework

2, 3, 5, 7, 11, 13, 17, 19, 23, 29, 31, 37, 41, 43, 47, 53, 59, 61, 67, 71, 73, 79, 83, 89, 97, 101, 103, 107, 109, 113, 127, 131, 137, 139, 149, 151, 157, 163, 167, 173, 179, 181, 191, 193, 197, and 199

Discovery Assignment Book (p. 177)

Home Practice†

Part 2. Going to the Theater

1. Friday–125, Saturday–144, Sunday–130

2. Friday–$1584, Saturday–$1771, Sunday–$1570

3. 320 − 79 = 241

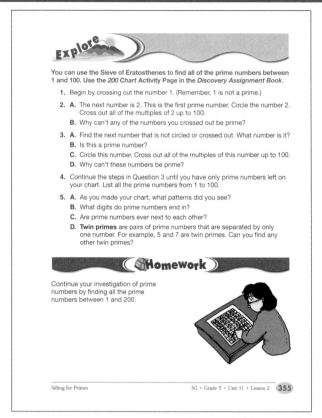

Student Guide - page 355

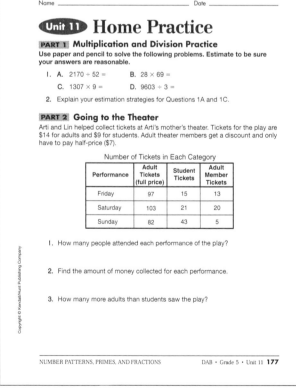

Discovery Assignment Book - page 177

*Answers and/or discussion are included in the Lesson Guide.
†Answers for all the Home Practice in the *Discovery Assignment Book* are at the end of the unit.

Lesson 3

Patterns with Square Numbers

Estimated Class Sessions

2

Lesson Overview

Students build squares from square-inch tiles and examine the patterns that develop among square numbers. They graph their data and find that the points do not form a straight line. They discover a relationship between square numbers and odd numbers.

Key Content

- Identifying square numbers.
- Identifying and describing number patterns.
- Using number patterns to solve problems.
- Making and interpreting point graphs (curves).
- Using variables in formulas.

Key Vocabulary

- formula

Math Facts

DPP item I reviews the division facts for the 3s and 9s.

Materials List

Supplies and Copies

Student	Teacher
Supplies for Each Student Pair	**Supplies**
• 25 square-inch tiles	
Copies	**Copies/Transparencies**
• 1 copy of *Three-column Data Table* per student (*Unit Resource Guide* Page 32)	• 1 transparency of *Three-column Data Table*, optional (*Unit Resource Guide* Page 32)
• 1 copy of *Centimeter Grid Paper* per student (*Unit Resource Guide* Page 53)	• 1 transparency of *Centimeter Grid Paper* (*Unit Resource Guide* Page 53)
• 1 copy of *Centimeter Graph Paper* per student (*Unit Resource Guide* Page 54)	• 1 transparency of *Centimeter Graph Paper*, optional (*Unit Resource Guide* Page 54)

All blackline masters including assessment, transparency, and DPP masters are also on the Teacher Resource CD.

Student Books

Patterns with Square Numbers (*Student Guide* Pages 356–359)

Daily Practice and Problems and Home Practice

DPP items G–J (*Unit Resource Guide* Pages 16–17)

Note: Classrooms whose pacing differs significantly from the suggested pacing of the units should use the Math Facts Calendar in Section 4 of the *Facts Resource Guide* to ensure students receive the complete math facts program.

Suggestions for using the DPPs are on page 51.

G. Bit: What's the Probability (URG p. 16)

Lin rolls a number cube. The six faces show the numbers 1, 2, 3, 4, 5, and 6. The probability that she will roll an even number is $\frac{3}{6}$ (or $\frac{1}{2}$) since she has 3 ways (2, 4, 6) to roll an even number out of 6 possible numbers. What is the probability that she will roll:

A. a prime number?

B. a factor of 6?

H. Task: Decimals to Fractions
(URG p. 16)

Express the following decimals as fractions. Reduce the fractions to lowest terms.

A. 0.25   B. 0.6

C. 0.35   D. 0.004

E. 0.068   F. 0.128

I. Bit: Division Practice II
(URG p. 17)

A. $810 \div 90 =$ B. $300 \div 30 =$

C. $6300 \div 70 =$ D. $180 \div 20 =$

E. $2100 \div 70 =$ F. $6000 \div 20 =$

G. $900 \div 30 =$ H. $900 \div 10 =$

I. $540 \div 90 =$

J. Challenge: Prime Factors
(URG p. 17)

Use the Sieve of Eratosthenes to find all the prime numbers between 301 and 320. Use your calculator as needed.

301	302	303	304	305
306	307	308	309	310
311	312	313	314	315
316	317	318	319	320

Count out and put the tiles into plastic bags. With 25 tiles each, students can build their own small squares and can combine tiles with other students' tiles to get the 100 tiles needed to build the large squares. For this reason, groups of four students work well for this activity.

Teaching the Activity

Part 1 Investigating Patterns

A somewhat surprising fact is that every square number is the sum of consecutive odd numbers. For example, $25 = 1 + 3 + 5 + 7 + 9$. In this activity, students will build squares with square-inch tiles and examine this and related facts about square numbers. It is not as important that students memorize the relationship between square numbers and odd numbers as it is that they experience the process of looking for and using patterns.

The questions on the *Patterns with Square Numbers* Activity Pages in the *Student Guide* structure this investigation so students can discover and explore the patterns themselves. First, they collect their data. In *Question 1,* students build squares using square-inch tiles, up to a size of at least 10×10. Each square is made by adding a band of tiles along the top and one side of the old square, as in Figure 4. For each square, students record the number of tiles on a side *(N)*, the number of tiles in the band that is added to the old square *(A)*, and the total number of tiles in the square *(T)*. They can use a *Three-column Data Table* to record their data. A completed data table is shown in Figure 5.

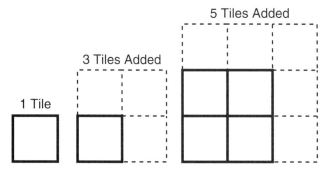

Figure 4: *Building new squares from old by adding tiles along top and side*

This activity allows students to look for patterns, explain why the patterns hold, and use them to solve problems. This is the kind of work mathematicians often do: they observe patterns among small easy-to-work-with numbers to explain (or "prove") why these patterns hold for these numbers, and generalize them to numbers they haven't examined. They then apply the patterns to solve problems about large numbers.

Patterns with Square Numbers

1. Use tiles to build squares of different sizes, as shown, up to at least a 10 × 10 square. As you build each square, record the data in a table like the one shown below.

1 × 1 square   2 × 2 square   3 × 3 square

N Number of Tiles on Each Side of Square	A Number of Tiles Added	T Total Number of Tiles
1	1	1
2	3	4
3	5	
4		
5		

2. Graph your data. Write *N*, the number of tiles on each side of a square, on the horizontal axis. Write *T*, the total number of tiles, on the vertical axis.
   - If your points lie on a straight line, draw the line.
   - If your points do not lie on a straight line, draw a curve that goes through all the points.

3. Look at your data table. Describe any patterns you see.
   - Look down the columns.
   - Look across the rows. Look from one row to the next.
   - Try to find patterns that use addition, subtraction, multiplication, or division.

Student Guide - page 356 (Answers on p. 55)

N Number of Tiles on Each Side of Square	A Number of Tiles Added	T Total Number of Tiles
1	1	1
2	3	4
3	5	9
4	7	16
5	9	25
6	11	36
7	13	49
8	15	64
9	17	⑧①
10	+ ⑲	100

81 + 19 = 100

Figure 5: *Completed data table*

TIMS Tip

Ask students why they think "square numbers" have the name they do. They will probably note the connection between the name and the squares they are building. (Students might enjoy asking their parents this question. Many adults never had this connection pointed out when they were children.)

Content Note

A **square number** is a number that is a product of a whole number multiplied by itself. Nine is a square number since $3 \times 3 = 9$. Square numbers can be represented by square arrays as shown below.

Note that we can write $3 \times 3 = 9$ as $3^2 = 9$. We read 3^2 as "three to the second power" or "three squared."

In **Question 2,** students graph their data. This graph is different from many of the others they have seen because the points do not lie on a straight line. Sometimes when data points from an experiment do not fall on a straight line, we fit a "best-fit line" through points, assuming that experimental error is the reason the points aren't exactly on a line. But in this activity, the numbers are exact. Unless students counted incorrectly, there was no experimental error. The points do not lie on a line, and we shouldn't force them to. The graph of the data is shown in Figure 6.

Question 3 asks students to look for patterns in their tables. Encourage them to use examples as they describe their patterns. Possible patterns include:

- The middle column is a list of the odd numbers.
- The third column is a list of the square numbers.
- The number in the third column *(T)* is the number in the first column multiplied by itself ($25 = 5 \times 5$).
- The number in the second column is twice the number in the first column minus one ($9 = 2 \times 5 - 1$).
- If you subtract a number in the third column from the number below it, you get a number in the second column ($25 - 16 = 9$).

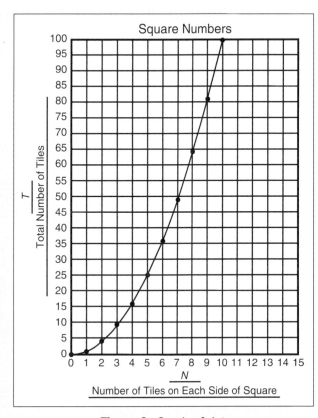

Figure 6: *Graph of data*

Question 4 asks students how they can get the next value of T (the total number of tiles in a square) without actually counting all the tiles. Use the following discussion prompts if students need hints for this question:

- *How can you use multiplication to find* T? (The value of T in row N is $N \times N$ or N^2. For example, the value of T in the 10th row is 10×10.)

- *How can you find* T *by using numbers from the second and third columns?* (To find T in row N, add the T in the previous row to A in row N. For example, the value of T in the 10th row is 100, which is the sum of 81, the value of T in row 9, and 19, the value of A in row 10.) This is illustrated in the Figure 5 table.

In **Question 5,** students write a formula to describe the patterns they observed. They write $T = N \times N$.

Students further investigate, in **Question 6,** the relationship between square numbers and odd numbers that appears in the patterns of **Questions 3–5.** Students examine the size of the band of tiles they added to build a square from the one before it. Figure 7 shows that the number of tiles in the band is always 2 times the number of tiles along a side of the square (these go on the top and side of the new square), minus 1 for the corner that is counted twice (since it is on both the top and the side). This is illustrated for a 5×5 square in the *Student Guide.* Students draw a similar diagram for an 11×11 square in **Question 6A.**

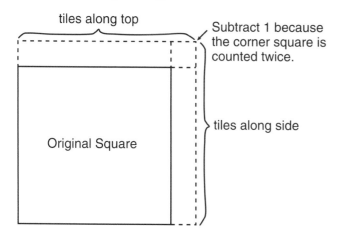

Figure 7: *Building a new square by adding a band of tiles to an old square*

Student Guide - page 357 *(Answers on p. 55)*

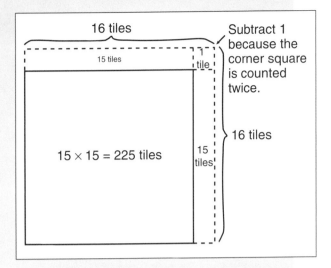

16 tiles

15 tiles

1 tile

Subtract 1 because the corner square is counted twice.

16 tiles

$15 \times 15 = 225$ tiles

15 tiles

Figure 8: *Finding 16×16 from 15×15*

Question 6B asks students to write a formula for finding A, the number of tiles added, using N, the number of tiles on a side. Students can write $A = N + N - 1$ or $A = 2 \times N - 1$.

Students use the pattern they found in **Question 6A** to find the square of larger numbers. For example, in **Question 6D**, students are given the fact that $15 \times 15 = 225$ and asked to find 16×16. This is illustrated in Figure 8. It can be computed as follows:

total tiles	=	old tiles	+	new tiles
16×16	=	15×15	+	$(16 + 16 - 1)$
	=	225	+	31
	=	256		

Part 2 Challenge Questions (optional)

Questions 7–8 are challenge questions that deal with the fact that squares are the sums of odd numbers. For example, $6 \times 6 = 1 + 3 + 5 + 7 + 9 + 11$. The first number in the sum is always 1. In **Question 7C**, students find a pattern that helps them find the last number in the sum. If they examine their lists of squares, they will find a pattern:

2^2 is $1 + 3$; the last number (3) is $2 \times 2 - 1$.
3^2 is $1 + 3 + 5$; the last number (5) is $2 \times 3 - 1$.
4^2 is $1 + 3 + 5 + 7$; the last number (7) is $2 \times 4 - 1$.
5^2 is $1 + 3 + 5 + 7 + 9$; the last number (9) is $2 \times 5 - 1$.

If they generalize this pattern, they may be able to conclude that:

The square of a number is the sum of the odd numbers from 1 to twice the number, minus 1, i.e., $N^2 = 1 + 3 + 5 \ldots + 2 \times N - 1$.

Using this pattern, they determine in **Question 7D** that 14^2 is the sum of the odd numbers from 1 to $2 \times 14 - 1 = 27$. In **Question 7E**, they use the pattern to find that 50^2 is the sum of the odd numbers from 1 to $2 \times 50 - 1 = 99$.

Some students may find other patterns. For example, another way to get the last number is to subtract 1 from the number being squared, double the result, and then add 1. Using this method, the last number in the sum for 50^2 is $2 \times 49 + 1 = 99$. This is the same number, but found using a different pattern.

Challenge Questions

7. A. On a piece of grid paper, draw a picture like this—up to at least 10×10. Write the size of the square inside before drawing the next larger one, as shown here.

$5 \times 5 = 25$
$4 \times 4 = 16$
$3 \times 3 = 9$
$2 \times 2 = 4$
1

B. Look back at the picture you drew in Question 7A. Use it to help you complete the following up to 10×10:
$1^2 = 1 \times 1 = 1 = 1$
$2^2 = 2 \times 2 = 1 + 3 = 4$
$3^2 = 3 \times 3 = 1 + 3 + 5 = 9$
$4^2 = 4 \times 4 = 1 + 3 + 5 + 7 = 16$
$5^2 = 5 \times 5 = 1 + 3 + 5 + 7 + 9 = 25$
$6^2 = 6 \times 6 = 1 + 3 + 5 + 7 + 9 + 11 = ?$

C. Every square number is the sum of odd numbers. The first number in the sum is 1. Do you see a pattern that lets you know what the last number in the sum is? Describe the pattern.

D. Use the pattern from Part C to write 14^2 as the sum of odd numbers.

E. Use this pattern to write 50^2 as the sum of odd numbers. What is the last number in the sum?

Student Guide - page 358 (Answers on p. 56)

In *Question 8,* students find sums of odd numbers. They can use the pattern from *Question 7,* but in reverse. For example, in *Question 8B,* they find the sum of the odd numbers from 1 to 25. This is the square of some mystery number. They found in *Question 7* that the last number in the list, 25, is twice the mystery number, minus 1. To get the mystery number back, they could add back the 1, getting 26, and then divide by 2, getting 13. The mystery number is 13. So the sum of the odd numbers from 1 to 25 is 13^2, or 169.

Another way is to note a different pattern:

1×1 is the sum of the first odd number
2×2 is the sum of the first 2 odd numbers
3×3 is the sum of the first 3 odd numbers
4×4 is the sum of the first 4 odd numbers
5×5 is the sum of the first 5 odd numbers.

To find the sum of the odd numbers from 1 to 25, we need to know how many odd numbers there are in the list. Since the odd numbers from 1 to 25 make up half of the numbers from 1 to 26 and since half of 26 is 13, there are 13 odd numbers from 1 to 25. The sum of the first 13 odd numbers is 13×13, or 169.

Math Facts

DPP Bit I reviews the division facts for the 3s and 9s using multiples of 10.

Homework and Practice

Assign DPP items G–J. Bit G reviews probability and Task H reviews fractions. Challenge J extends students' number sense for primes and composites.

Extension

The Challenge Questions section in the *Student Guide* extends the activity so students can identify and apply more complex patterns.

Literature Connection

Hulme, Joy. *Sea Squares.* Hyperion Books for Children, New York, 1993. This book develops square number facts through counting.

8. If you add odd numbers in order, starting with 1, you will always get a square number. Look for a pattern in your list from Question 7B. Describe that pattern, then use it to:

   A. Find the sum of the odd numbers from 1 to 19.

   B. Find the sum of the odd numbers from 1 to 25.

   C. Find the sum of the odd numbers from 1 to 99.

Patterns with Square Numbers   SG • Grade 5 • Unit 11 • Lesson 3   **359**

Student Guide - page 359 (Answers on p. 56)

The Importance of Proving Patterns. To prove something true mathematically, it is not enough to observe it true for the first few numbers we try. Some patterns hold for a few smaller numbers, but not for larger ones. But, by showing a way any square can be built from a smaller square, we did more than just observe the patterns. Our constructions showed that the next square always comes by adding an odd number and it even showed how to find the odd number. This is stronger than just observing the pattern that works for the first few square numbers. It proved that the pattern works for all squares.

At a Glance

Math Facts and Daily Practice and Problems

DPP item I reviews the division facts for the 3s and 9s. Items G and H review probability and fractions. Challenge J extends students' understanding of prime and composite numbers.

Part 1. Investigating Patterns

1. Distribute 25 square-inch tiles to each student.
2. Students build squares, up to at least a 10 x 10 square, building larger squares from smaller ones. They record data in a *Three-column Data Table* (**Question 1** in the *Patterns with Square Numbers* Activity Pages in the *Student Guide*).
3. Students graph their data **(Question 2)**. The result is a curve, not a straight line.
4. Students look for patterns in their data tables and find a relationship between square numbers and odd numbers. **(Questions 3–4)**
5. Students write formulas for the square numbers in the third column. **(Question 5)**
6. Students examine the method of building larger squares from smaller squares. This gives a visual model of the relationship between the square numbers and the odd numbers they explored in **Questions 3–4.** They use this pattern to solve problems. **(Question 6)**

Part 2. Challenge Questions (optional)

1. Students are challenged to find a pattern that lets them express a square as the sum of odd numbers. They use this pattern to solve problems. **(Question 7)**
2. Students use their patterns to find the sums of odd numbers. **(Question 8)**

Extension

Use the Challenge Questions in the *Student Guide* to extend the lesson.

Connection

Read and discuss *Sea Squares* by Joy Hulme.

Answer Key is on pages 55–56.

Notes:

Name _____ Date _____

Centimeter Grid Paper

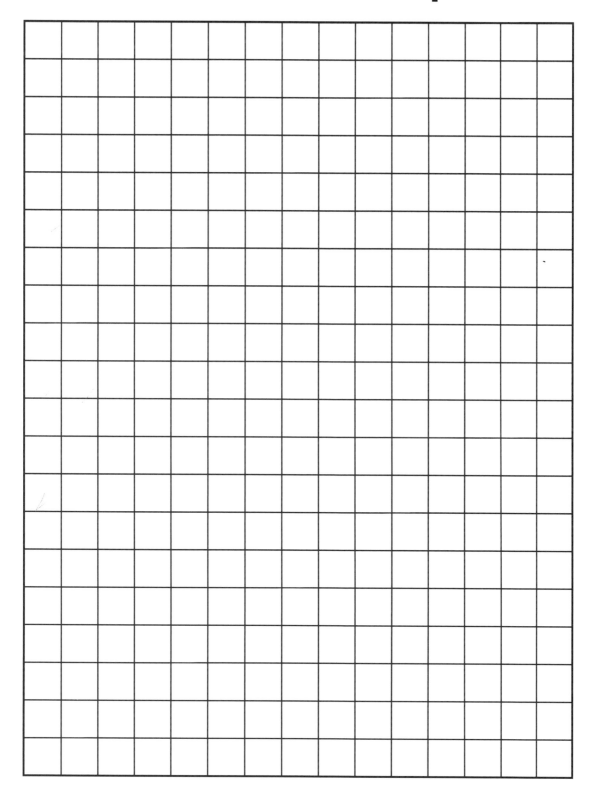

Name _____ Date _____

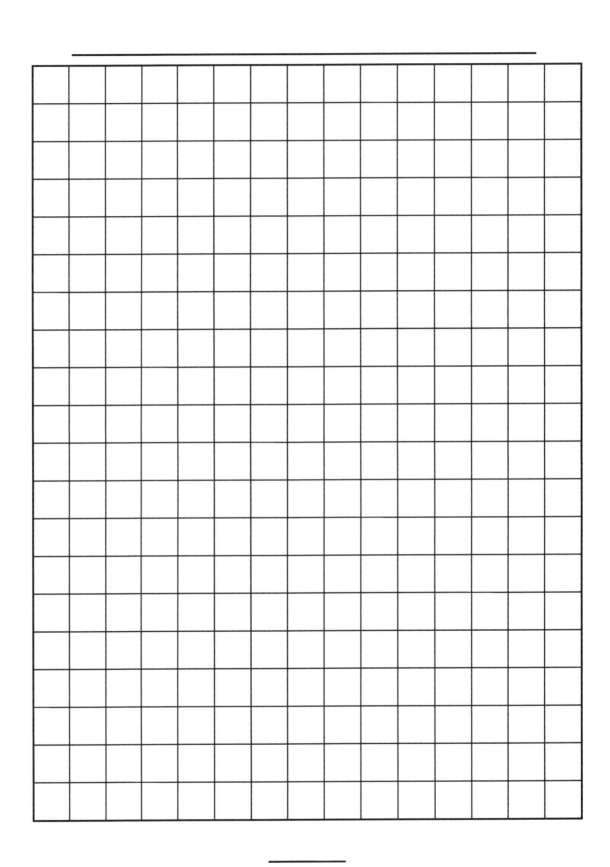

Centimeter Graph Paper, Blackline Master

Student Guide (p. 356)

Patterns with Square Numbers

1. See Figure 5 in Lesson Guide 3.*

2. See Figure 6 in Lesson Guide 3.*

3. Answers may vary. Possible patterns include: All the numbers in the second column are odd numbers. All the numbers in the third column are square numbers. The numbers in the third column are the corresponding number in the first column multiplied by itself. T is found by adding the A in the same row to the T in the previous row. Subtracting the two numbers above and below one another in the third column gives a number in the second column.*

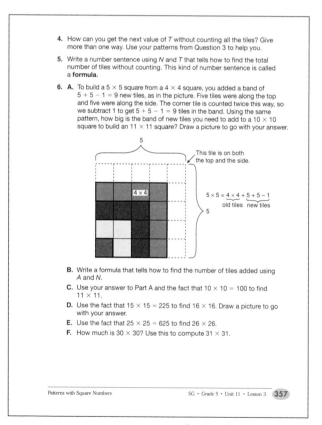

Patterns with Square Numbers

1. Use tiles to build squares of different sizes, as shown, up to at least a 10×10 square. As you build each square, record the data in a table like the one shown below.

1 × 1 square   2 × 2 square   3 × 3 square

N Number of Tiles on Each Side of Square	A Number of Tiles Added	T Total Number of Tiles
1	1	1
2	3	4
3	5	
4		
5		

2. Graph your data. Write N, the number of tiles on each side of a square, on the horizontal axis. Write T, the total number of tiles, on the vertical axis.
   • If your points lie on a straight line, draw the line.
   • If your points do not lie on a straight line, draw a curve that goes through all the points.

3. Look at your data table. Describe any patterns you see.
   • Look down the columns.
   • Look across the rows. Look from one row to the next.
   • Try to find patterns that use addition, subtraction, multiplication, or division.

356   SG • Grade 5 • Unit 11 • Lesson 3   Patterns with Square Numbers

Student Guide - page 356

Student Guide (p. 357)

4. The next value of T will be the next square number which is $11^2 = 121$. We can get the next T value by adding 100 to the next odd number in the second column (21) so: $100 + 21 = 121$.*

5. $T = N \times N$*

6. See Figure 7 in Lesson Guide 3.*

   A. $11 + 11 - 1$ or $2 \times 11 - 1$

   B. $A = 2 \times N - 1$ or $A = N + N - 1$

   C. $11 \times 11 = 100 + 11 + 11 - 1 = 121$

   D. $16 \times 16 = 225 + 16 + 16 - 1 = 256$

   E. $26 \times 26 = 625 + 26 + 26 - 1 = 676$

   F. $30 \times 30 = 900; 31 \times 31 = 900 + 31 + 31 - 1 = 961$

4. How can you get the next value of T without counting all the tiles? Give more than one way. Use your patterns from Question 3 to help you.

5. Write a number sentence using N and T that tells how to find the total number of tiles without counting. This kind of number sentence is called a **formula**.

6. **A.** To build a 5×5 square from a 4×4 square, you added a band of $5 + 5 - 1 = 9$ new tiles, as in the picture. Five tiles were along the top and five were along the side. The corner tile is counted twice this way, so we subtract 1 to get $5 + 5 - 1 = 9$ tiles in the band. Using the same pattern, how big is the band of new tiles you need to add to a 10×10 square to build an 11×11 square? Draw a picture to go with your answer.

This tile is on both the top and the side.

$5 \times 5 = \underbrace{4 \times 4}_{\text{old tiles}} + \underbrace{5 + 5 - 1}_{\text{new tiles}}$

   B. Write a formula that tells how to find the number of tiles added using A and N.
   C. Use your answer to Part A and the fact that $10 \times 10 = 100$ to find 11×11.
   D. Use the fact that $15 \times 15 = 225$ to find 16×16. Draw a picture to go with your answer.
   E. Use the fact that $25 \times 25 = 625$ to find 26×26.
   F. How much is 30×30? Use this to compute 31×31.

Patterns with Square Numbers   SG • Grade 5 • Unit 11 • Lesson 3   357

Student Guide - page 357

*Answers and/or discussion are included in the Lesson Guide.

Challenge Questions

7. **A.** On a piece of grid paper, draw a picture like this—up to at least 10 × 10. Write the size of the square inside before drawing the next larger one, as shown here.

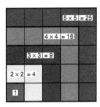

B. Look back at the picture you drew in Question 7A. Use it to help you complete the following up to 10 × 10:

$1^2 = 1 \times 1 = 1 = 1$
$2^2 = 2 \times 2 = 1 + 3 = 4$
$3^2 = 3 \times 3 = 1 + 3 + 5 = 9$
$4^2 = 4 \times 4 = 1 + 3 + 5 + 7 = 16$
$5^2 = 5 \times 5 = 1 + 3 + 5 + 7 + 9 = 25$
$6^2 = 6 \times 6 = 1 + 3 + 5 + 7 + 9 + 11 = ?$

C. Every square number is the sum of odd numbers. The first number in the sum is 1. Do you see a pattern that lets you know what the last number in the sum is? Describe the pattern.

D. Use the pattern from Part C to write 14^2 as the sum of odd numbers.

E. Use this pattern to write 50^2 as the sum of odd numbers. What is the last number in the sum?

Student Guide - page 358

8. If you add odd numbers in order, starting with 1, you will always get a square number. Look for a pattern in your list from Question 7B. Describe that pattern, then use it to:

A. Find the sum of the odd numbers from 1 to 19.
B. Find the sum of the odd numbers from 1 to 25.
C. Find the sum of the odd numbers from 1 to 99.

Student Guide - page 359

Student Guide (p. 358)

7. **B.** $6^2 = 6 \times 6 = 1 + 3 + 5 + 7 + 9 + 11 = 36$

$7^2 = 7 \times 7 = 1 + 3 + 5 + 7 + 9 + 11 + 13 = 49$

$8^2 = 8 \times 8 = 1 + 3 + 5 + 7 + 9 + 11 + 13 + 15 = 64$

$9^2 = 9 \times 9 = 1 + 3 + 5 + 7 + 9 + 11 + 13 + 15 + 17 = 81$

$10^2 = 10 \times 10 = 1 + 3 + 5 + 7 + 9 + 11 + 13 + 15 + 17 + 19 = 100$

C. The last number in the sum is two times the number minus 1. Therefore, every square number, N^2, is the sum of odd numbers from 1 to $2N - 1$.*

D. 14^2 will be the sum of all odd numbers from 1 to $2(14) - 1 = 27$. $14^2 = 1 + 3 + 5 + 7 + 9 + 11 + 13 + 15 + 17 + 19 + 21 + 23 + 25 + 27 = 196$*

E. 50^2 will be the sum of all odd numbers from 1 to $2(50) - 1 = 99$. The last number in the sum is 99.*

Student Guide (p. 359)

8. A square number is the sum of all odd numbers from 1 to two times the number minus 1. Therefore, the sum of a list of odd numbers in order can be found using the reverse of this pattern. Adding 1 to the last number in the sum and dividing by 2 will give the number to be squared.

A. Since the last number in the sum is 19, the number to be squared is $(19 + 1) \div 2 = 20 \div 2 = 10$. Therefore, the sum of the odd numbers from 1 to 19 is $10^2 = 100$.

B. The number to be squared is $(25 + 1) \div 2 = 26 \div 2 = 13$. Therefore, the sum of the odd numbers from 1 to 25 is $13^2 = 169$.*

C. The number to be squared is $(99 + 1) \div 2 = 100 \div 2 = 50$. Therefore, the sum of the odd numbers from 1 to 99 is $50^2 = 2500$.

*Answers and/or discussion are included in the Lesson Guide.

Lesson 4

Finding Prime Factors

Estimated Class Sessions

1-2

Lesson Overview

Students find the prime factors of numbers. Strategies include using known factors, a factor tree, and calculators. Students rewrite numbers as a product of their prime factors using exponents.

Key Content

- Finding the prime factorization of a number.
- Using exponents.

Key Vocabulary

- exponent
- factor tree
- prime factorization

Homework

Assign **Questions 1–4** in the Homework section in the *Student Guide*.

Assessment

Use Part 3 of the Home Practice to assess students' fluency with factors, exponents, and prime numbers.

Curriculum Sequence

Before This Unit

In Grade 4, students found prime factors using factor trees in Unit 4 Lesson 4. They also learned divisibility rules in Grade 4 Unit 7 Lesson 2. Students used exponents in Grade 4 in Unit 4 Lesson 4. In Grade 5, they used exponents in Unit 2.

Materials List

Supplies and Copies

Student	Teacher
Supplies for Each Student • calculator	**Supplies**
Copies	**Copies/Transparencies** • 2–3 blank transparencies, optional

All blackline masters including assessment, transparency, and DPP masters are also on the Teacher Resource CD.

Student Books

Finding Prime Factors (*Student Guide* Pages 360–362)
Factor Trees (*Discovery Assignment Book* Page 185), optional

Daily Practice and Problems and Home Practice

DPP items K–L (*Unit Resource Guide* Pages 17–18)
Home Practice Part 3 (*Discovery Assignment Book* Page 178)

Note: Classrooms whose pacing differs significantly from the suggested pacing of the units should use the Math Facts Calendar in Section 4 of the *Facts Resource Guide* to ensure students receive the complete math facts program.

Daily Practice and Problems

Suggestions for using the DPPs are on page 62.

K. Bit: Division (URG p. 17)

Solve using paper and pencil. Estimate to be sure your answers are reasonable.

1. $5600 \div 80 =$
2. $5973 \div 78 =$
3. $48,000 \div 60 =$
4. $47,346 \div 61 =$

L. Task: Divisibility Rules (URG p. 18)

Tell which numbers below are divisible by 2. Tell which numbers below are divisible by 3. Remember, a number is divisible by 3 if the sum of its digits is divisible by 3.

A. 26   B. 258
C. 368   D. 939
E. 1032

Which numbers above are divisible by 6? Write the divisibility rule for 6.

You may wish to use DPP Task L as a warm-up.

Read Mr. Moreno's challenge to his class on the *Finding Prime Factors* Activity Pages in the *Student Guide.* Discuss student responses to this challenge. Students can work together to find the additional information asked for in *Questions 1–2.* Collect students' responses on the board or blank transparencies.

Question 3 describes Brandon's use of a **factor tree** to find the prime factors of 144. Use this question to review prime factorization and factor trees. If this is the first time students are seeing factor trees or if they need to review, have them complete the *Factor Trees* Activity Page in the *Discovery Assignment Book* in which they factor smaller numbers.

Question 3A provides students with practice making a factor tree. One strategy for starting a factor tree is to identify the smallest prime number by which the number is divisible. For example, to find the smallest prime factor of 144, students can use a calculator or divisibility rules. Students should be able to identify this number as 2. Once they identify this prime

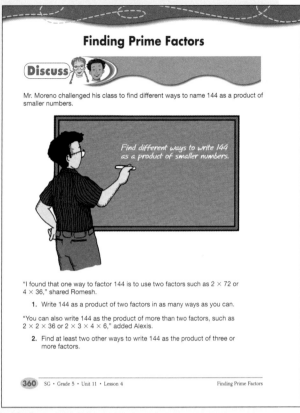

Student Guide - page 360 *(Answers on p. 64)*

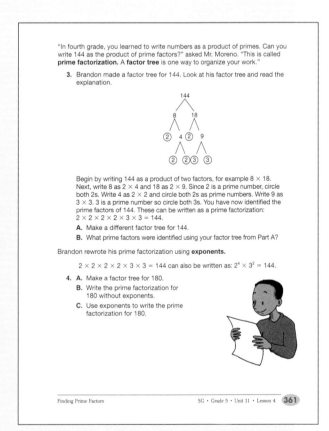

Student Guide - page 361 *(Answers on p. 64)*

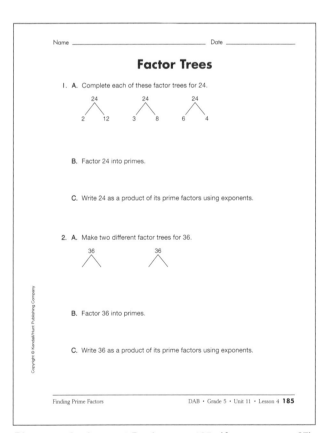

Discovery Assignment Book - page 185 *(Answers on p. 67)*

factor, they can use their calculators or other methods to divide 144 by 2 and find the other number in this factor pair, in this case, 72. Students can record this pair of factors in their factor trees for 144, as in Figure 9.

Students can now continue their factor trees by finding a pair of factors for 72. Students should be able to identify factors for 72 without using their calculators. However, if they can't, they can use the same procedure as before to find factors of 72. Have students complete the factor tree for 144. One possible tree is shown in Figure 10.

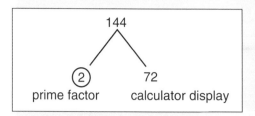

Figure 9: *Starting a factor tree for 144*

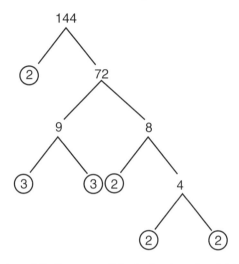

Figure 10: *One possible factor tree for 144*

After completing **Question 3B,** students should realize that even though there may be many different ways to make a factor tree for a number, they will always end up with the same prime factors (though they may be in a different order).

Once students have made factor trees, they can write numbers as products of their prime factors. This is called **prime factorization.** Students make a factor tree and write a prime factorization using exponents in **Question 4.** You may need to review exponents with students.

Questions 5–6 introduce the use of the exponent key on the scientific calculator. Students can use this key to check their prime factorizations written with exponents. Exponent keys are labeled differently on different scientific calculators. Possible labels include:

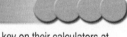

Help students identify the exponent key on their calculators.

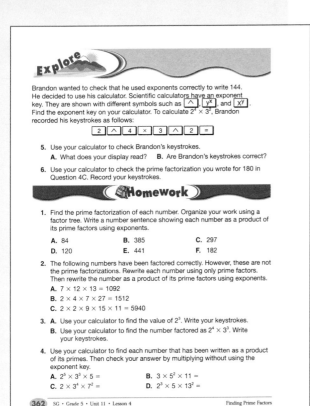

Student Guide - page 362 *(Answers on pp. 65–66)*

Homework and Practice

- Students complete *Questions 1–4* in the Homework section in the *Student Guide*.

- DPP item K provides practice with 2-digit division. Use DPP Task L to review students' understanding of the divisibility rules.

Assessment

Use Part 3 of the Home Practice to assess students' understanding of prime numbers, factors, and exponents.

Answers for Part 3 of the Home Practice are in the Answer Key at the end of this lesson and at the end of this unit.

Resources

The Largest Known Primes Web Site (http://www.utm.edu/research/primes/largest.html)

Name _____ Date _____

PART 3 **Using Exponents**

1. Each of the three numbers below is written as a product of primes. Rewrite the prime factorizations using exponents.

   A. $180 = 2 \times 3 \times 5 \times 2 \times 3 =$ _____

   B. $2125 = 5 \times 17 \times 5 \times 5 =$ _____

   C. $17,820 = 11 \times 2 \times 3 \times 3 \times 5 \times 2 \times 3 \times 3 =$ _____

2. Write each of the following numbers as a product of its primes without exponents. Use factor trees. Then write the number as a product of its primes using exponents.

   A. 20   B. 48   C. 56

PART 4 **Fractions**

1. Reduce the following fractions to lowest terms.

   A. $\frac{14}{28}$ B. $\frac{24}{42}$ C. $\frac{60}{200}$ D. $\frac{27}{90}$ E. $\frac{57}{120}$

2. Solve the following. First, find common denominators and then add or subtract. Reduce your answers to lowest terms.

   A. $\frac{4}{5} - \frac{3}{10} =$ B. $\frac{2}{5} - \frac{1}{15} =$ C. $\frac{5}{6} + \frac{1}{24} =$

178 DAB · Grade 5 · Unit 11   NUMBER PATTERNS, PRIMES, AND FRACTIONS

Discovery Assignment Book - page 178 *(Answers on p. 66)*

At a Glance

Math Facts and Daily Practice and Problems

DPP item K provides division practice. Task L reviews the divisibility rules.

Teaching the Activity

1. Read Mr. Moreno's challenge to his class on the *Finding Prime Factors* Activity Pages in the *Student Guide.*
2. Discuss student solutions to *Questions 1–2.*
3. Ask students to provide additional examples of how to factor 144 in both *Questions 1–2.*
4. Introduce factor trees using *Question 3.* If students need additional practice, use the *Factor Trees* Activity Page in the *Discovery Assignment Book.*
5. Complete *Questions 4–6* reviewing exponents and exploring the exponent key.

Homework

Assign *Questions 1–4* in the Homework section in the *Student Guide.*

Assessment

Use Part 3 of the Home Practice to assess students' fluency with factors, exponents, and prime numbers.

Answer Key is on pages 64–67.

Notes:

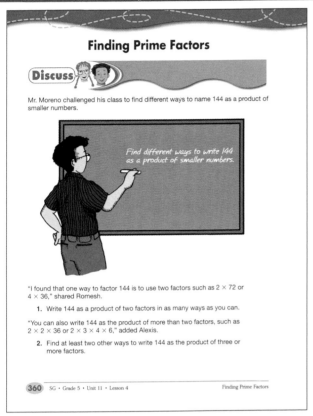

Student Guide - page 360

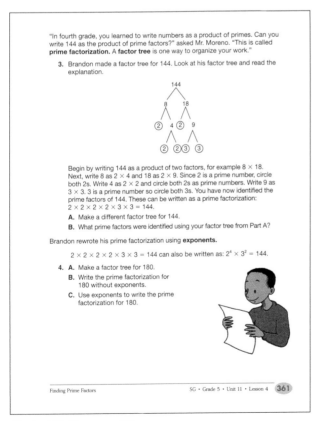

Student Guide - page 361

Student Guide (pp. 360–361)

Finding Prime Factors

1. 2×72; 3×48; 4×36; 6×24; 8×18; 9×16; 12×12

2. Answers will vary. Two possible solutions are: $2 \times 3 \times 3 \times 8$; $2 \times 2 \times 2 \times 3 \times 6$

3. **A.** Answers will vary. One possible solution is given below.*

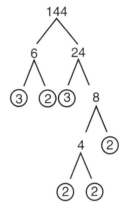

   B. $3 \times 2 \times 3 \times 2 \times 2 \times 2 = 144$

4. **A.** Answers will vary. One possible solution is given below.

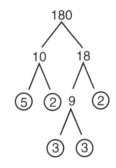

   B. $2 \times 2 \times 3 \times 3 \times 5 = 180$
   C. $2^2 \times 3^2 \times 5 = 180$

*Answers and/or discussion are included in the Lesson Guide.

Student Guide (p. 362)

5. A.*  144

B. Yes; since the display reads 144, Brandon's keystrokes are correct.

6.*  2 y^X 2 × 3 y^X 2 × 5 =

180

Calculator displays may vary.

Homework

1. Factor trees will vary. One possible tree is shown for each.

A. $2^2 \times 3 \times 7 = 84$

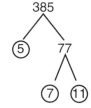

B. $5 \times 7 \times 11 = 385$

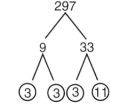

C. $3^3 \times 11 = 297$

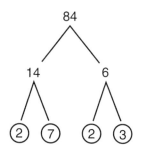

D. $2^3 \times 3 \times 5 = 120$

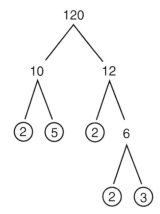

E. $3^2 \times 7^2 = 441$

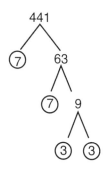

F. $2 \times 7 \times 13 = 182$

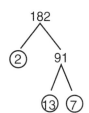

Brandon wanted to check that he used exponents correctly to write 144. He decided to use his calculator. Scientific calculators have an exponent key. They are shown with different symbols such as $\boxed{\wedge}$, $\boxed{y^X}$, and $\boxed{x^y}$. Find the exponent key on your calculator. To calculate $2^4 \times 3^2$, Brandon recorded his keystrokes as follows:

2 $\wedge$ 4 × 3 $\wedge$ 2 =

5. Use your calculator to check Brandon's keystrokes.
   A. What does your display read?   **B.** Are Brandon's keystrokes correct?

6. Use your calculator to check the prime factorization you wrote for 180 in Question 4C. Record your keystrokes.

Homework

1. Find the prime factorization of each number. Organize your work using a factor tree. Write a number sentence showing each number as a product of its prime factors using exponents.

   A. 84   **B.** 385   **C.** 297
   D. 120   **E.** 441   **F.** 182

2. The following numbers have been factored correctly. However, these are not the prime factorizations. Rewrite each number using only prime factors. Then rewrite the number as a product of its prime factors using exponents.
   A. $7 \times 12 \times 13 = 1092$
   B. $2 \times 4 \times 7 \times 27 = 1512$
   C. $2 \times 2 \times 9 \times 15 \times 11 = 5940$

3. **A.** Use your calculator to find the value of 2^3. Write your keystrokes.
   B. Use your calculator to find the number factored as $2^4 \times 3^3$. Write your keystrokes.

4. Use your calculator to find each number that has been written as a product of its primes. Then check your answer by multiplying without using the exponent key.
   A. $2^5 \times 3^3 \times 5 =$ **B.** $3 \times 5^2 \times 11 =$
   C. $2 \times 3^4 \times 7^2 =$ **D.** $2^3 \times 5 \times 13^2 =$

362   SG • Grade 5 • Unit 11 • Lesson 4   Finding Prime Factors

Student Guide - page 362

---

*Answers and/or discussion are included in the Lesson Guide.

2. **A.** $2 \times 2 \times 3 \times 7 \times 13 = 1092$

   $2^2 \times 3 \times 7 \times 13 = 1092$

   B. $2 \times 2 \times 2 \times 3 \times 3 \times 3 \times 7 = 1512$

   $2^3 \times 3^3 \times 7 = 1512$

   C. $2 \times 2 \times 3 \times 3 \times 3 \times 5 \times 11 = 5940$

   $2^2 \times 3^3 \times 5 \times 11 = 5940$

3. **A.** [2][yˣ][3][=][8.]

   B. [2][yˣ][4][×][3][yˣ][3][=]

   [432]

4. **A.** 4320   **B.** 825

   C. 7938   **D.** 6760

Discovery Assignment Book (p. 178)

Home Practice*

Part 3. Using Exponents

1. **A.** $180 = 2^2 \times 3^2 \times 5$

   B. $2125 = 5^3 \times 17$

   C. $17820 = 2^2 \times 3^4 \times 5 \times 11$

2. **A.** $20 = 5 \times 2 \times 2$

   $20 = 2^2 \times 5$

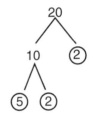

   B. $48 = 3 \times 2 \times 2 \times 2 \times 2$

   $48 = 2^4 \times 3$

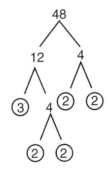

   C. $56 = 2 \times 2 \times 2 \times 7$

   $56 = 2^3 \times 7$

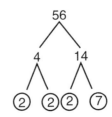

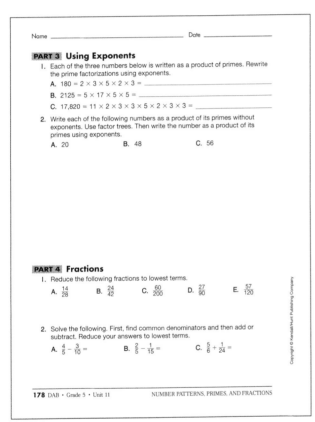

Name _____ Date _____

PART 3 Using Exponents

1. Each of the three numbers below is written as a product of primes. Rewrite the prime factorizations using exponents.

   A. $180 = 2 \times 3 \times 5 \times 2 \times 3 =$ _____

   B. $2125 = 5 \times 17 \times 5 \times 5 =$ _____

   C. $17,820 = 11 \times 2 \times 3 \times 3 \times 5 \times 2 \times 3 \times 3 =$ _____

2. Write each of the following numbers as a product of its primes without exponents. Use factor trees. Then write the number as a product of its primes using exponents.

   A. 20   B. 48   C. 56

PART 4 Fractions

1. Reduce the following fractions to lowest terms.

   A. $\frac{14}{28}$ B. $\frac{24}{42}$ C. $\frac{60}{200}$ D. $\frac{27}{90}$ E. $\frac{57}{120}$

2. Solve the following. First, find common denominators and then add or subtract. Reduce your answers to lowest terms.

   A. $\frac{4}{5} - \frac{3}{10} =$ B. $\frac{2}{5} - \frac{1}{15} =$ C. $\frac{5}{6} + \frac{1}{24} =$

178 DAB • Grade 5 • Unit 11   NUMBER PATTERNS, PRIMES, AND FRACTIONS

Discovery Assignment Book - page 178

*Answers for all the Home Practice in the *Discovery Assignment Book* are at the end of the unit.

Discovery Assignment Book (p. 185)

Factor Trees

1. **A.**

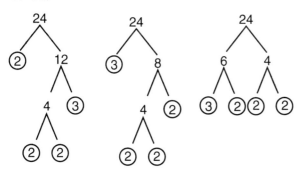

B. $2 \times 2 \times 2 \times 3$
C. $2^3 \times 3 = 24$

2. **A.**

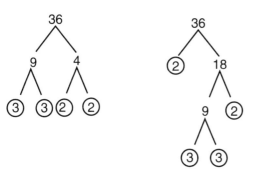

B. $2 \times 2 \times 3 \times 3$
C. $2^2 \times 3^2 = 36$

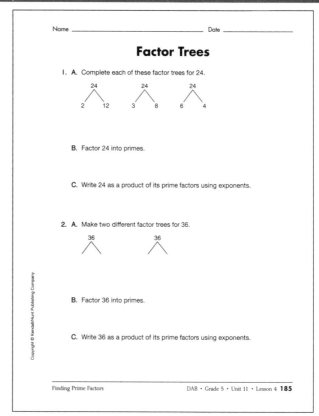

Discovery Assignment Book - page 185

Lesson 5

Comparing Fractions

Lesson Overview

Estimated Class Sessions
2

Students find common denominators and use them to compare fractions.

Key Content

- Finding common denominators.
- Comparing fractions using common denominators.

Key Vocabulary

- common denominator

Math Facts

DPP items M and P include a review of the division facts for the 3s and 9s.

Homework

1. Assign the questions in the Homework section.
2. Assign Part 5 of the Home Practice.

Assessment

1. Use DPP Task P as a quiz.
2. Use the *Observational Assessment Record* to note students' abilities to find common denominators and compare fractions.

Curriculum Sequence

Before This Unit

In Unit 5 Lessons 4 and 5, students used several strategies to compare fractions including finding common denominators using rectangles on dot paper. They also used benchmarks to compare fractions. In the lab *A Day at the Races* in Unit 5 Lesson 5, students used graphs and tables to compare ratios written as fractions.

After This Unit

Students work with fractions in Unit 12.

Materials List

Supplies and Copies

Student	Teacher
Supplies for Each Student	**Supplies**
Copies	**Copies/Transparencies**

All blackline masters including assessment, transparency, and DPP masters are also on the Teacher Resource CD.

Student Books
Comparing Fractions (*Student Guide* Pages 363–367)

Daily Practice and Problems and Home Practice
DPP items M–P (*Unit Resource Guide* Pages 18–19)
Home Practice Part 5 (*Discovery Assignment Book* Page 179)

Note: Classrooms whose pacing differs significantly from the suggested pacing of the units should use the Math Facts Calendar in Section 4 of the *Facts Resource Guide* to ensure students receive the complete math facts program.

Assessment Tools
Observational Assessment Record (*Unit Resource Guide* Pages 11–12)

Daily Practice and Problems

Suggestions for using the DPPs are on page 73.

M. Bit: Division Practice III
(URG p. 18)

A. $180 \div 6 =$

B. $270 \div 3 =$

C. $4500 \div 50 =$

D. $2400 \div 800 =$

E. $36,000 \div 40 =$

F. $90,000 \div 100 =$

N. Task: Practicing the Operations
(URG p. 18)

Solve the following problems using a paper-and-pencil method. Estimate to be sure your answers are reasonable.

1. A. $34 \times 93 =$ B. $3489 \div 13 =$

    C. $423 \times 9 =$ D. $0.43 \times 0.7 =$

    E. $0.23 \times 8 =$ F. $6086 \div 39 =$

2. Explain your estimation strategy for E.

O. Bit: Fractions (URG p. 19)

Find one number for n that makes each sentence true.

A. $\frac{1}{5} = \frac{n}{25}$ B. $\frac{6}{21} = \frac{2}{n}$

C. $\frac{n}{12} < \frac{3}{4}$ D. $\frac{7}{8} < \frac{n}{16}$

P. Task: Finding Factors
(URG p. 19)

1. Find all the factors for the following numbers. Tell which numbers are prime.

    A. 23   B. 258

    C. 39   D. 73

    E. 1278

2. Draw a factor tree for each composite number above. Then write its prime factorization.

Briefly review equivalent fractions, a topic discussed in Unit 3. Choose a fraction, for example, $\frac{2}{5}$, and ask:

- *Name three fractions equivalent to that fraction.* (Draw from students that we can multiply both the numerator and denominator of a fraction by the same number to get a fraction equivalent to the first.)

Use Bit O in the DPP to provide additional practice in finding equivalent fractions.

Teaching the Activity

Begin by asking the following questions:

- *Which is larger, $\frac{1}{12}$ or $\frac{9}{10}$?*
- *Which is larger, $\frac{1}{3}$ or $\frac{2}{3}$?*
- *Which is larger, $\frac{1}{2}$ or $\frac{1}{3}$?*

Ask students to explain their answers. For the first pair, they might use $\frac{1}{2}$ as a benchmark. Since $\frac{1}{12}$ is less than $\frac{1}{2}$ and $\frac{9}{10}$ is more than $\frac{1}{2}$, they can conclude that $\frac{1}{12} < \frac{9}{10}$. For the second pair, they can also use the benchmark method, or they might notice that these fractions are easy to compare because they have the same denominator. The third pair of fractions is also easy because they have the same numerator.

Next, ask students:

- *Which is larger, $\frac{2}{3}$ or $\frac{3}{4}$?*

Again, ask for reasons for their answers. This pair of fractions is more difficult to compare because both their numerators and denominators are different. The benchmark method isn't very helpful because both fractions are larger than $\frac{1}{2}$ and less than 1. Students might remember comparing fractions like this in Unit 5 Lesson 4. There they used rectangles on dot paper to help them find common denominators. Another method to compare these fractions is to use calculators to find decimals.

The vignette on the *Comparing Fractions* Activity Pages in the *Student Guide* tells of a situation in which John and his mother need to know which fraction, $\frac{2}{3}$ or $\frac{3}{4}$, is larger. It is followed by a discussion of common denominators. Students learn they can find a **common denominator** for two fractions by finding a number that is a multiple of both denominators. Have the class read the pages and answer *Questions 1–6* in small groups.

Comparing Fractions

Finding Equivalent Fractions

We learned in Unit 3 that when we multiply both the numerator and denominator of a fraction by the same number, we get a fraction that is equivalent to the first. For example, if we multiply both the numerator and denominator of $\frac{2}{3}$ by 5, we get the equivalent fraction $\frac{10}{15}$.

$$\frac{2}{3} = \frac{2 \times 5}{3 \times 5} = \frac{10}{15}$$

Sometimes it is helpful to find equivalent fractions when we want to compare fractions. Can you find three other fractions that are equivalent to $\frac{2}{3}$?

Comparing Fractions

John and his mother were shopping for ingredients to make cookies and fudge for the school bake sale.

"The cookie recipe calls for $\frac{1}{3}$ can of evaporated milk," said John. "After we make the cookies, we'll have $\frac{2}{3}$ of a can left over. I wonder whether that will be enough to make the fudge."

"The fudge recipe calls for $\frac{3}{4}$ can of evaporated milk," said his mother. "If $\frac{2}{3}$ is more than $\frac{3}{4}$, we'll have enough. Otherwise, we'll have to buy another can. Which do you think is larger, $\frac{2}{3}$ or $\frac{3}{4}$?"

Before solving John's problem, think about some other fractions:

Which is larger, $\frac{1}{3}$ or $\frac{2}{3}$?

It is easy to compare fractions that have the same denominator. Two-thirds is more than one-third, since two is more than one.

Which is larger, $\frac{1}{2}$ or $\frac{1}{3}$?

$\frac{1}{3}$ $\frac{2}{3}$

Student Guide - page 363

One-half is larger than one-third. Remember that when the numerators are equal, as they are here, the fraction with the smaller denominator is larger. When we cut the whole into 2 pieces, each piece is larger than when we cut the whole into 3 pieces.

$\frac{1}{2}$ $\frac{1}{3}$

Which is larger, $\frac{2}{3}$ or $\frac{3}{4}$?

This was John's problem. One way to compare fractions with different denominators is to find equivalent fractions with the same denominator.

To compare $\frac{2}{3}$ and $\frac{3}{4}$, John chose 12 as the denominator because it is a multiple of both 3 and 4. To compare $\frac{2}{3}$ and $\frac{3}{4}$, John renamed them so they had the same denominator (12).

$$\frac{2}{3} = \frac{2 \times 4}{3 \times 4} = \frac{8}{12} \qquad \frac{3}{4} = \frac{3 \times 3}{4 \times 3} = \frac{9}{12}$$

Since $\frac{8}{12} < \frac{9}{12}$, then $\frac{2}{3} < \frac{3}{4}$.

"I guess $\frac{2}{3}$ of a can isn't enough milk for the recipe that calls for $\frac{3}{4}$ can," said John. "We'll have to buy another can."

When fractions have the same denominator, we say they have **common denominators.** Twelve is a common denominator for $\frac{2}{3}$ and $\frac{3}{4}$. To find a common denominator for two fractions, we need to find a number that is a multiple of both denominators.

Student Guide - page 364

Discuss

1. Write each pair of fractions with a common denominator. Then compare the fractions. Use the symbols < or >.

   A. $\frac{1}{2}$ $\frac{3}{8}$ B. $\frac{5}{6}$ $\frac{7}{12}$

   C. $\frac{17}{20}$ $\frac{3}{4}$ D. $\frac{2}{3}$ $\frac{7}{9}$

One way to find a common denominator for two fractions is to multiply both denominators together. For example, a common denominator for $\frac{2}{3}$ and $\frac{4}{5}$ is 15. Since $3 \times 5 = 15$, we know that 15 is a multiple of both 3 and 5.

2. Which is larger? To answer, find common denominators and compare.

   A. $\frac{4}{5}$ or $\frac{2}{3}$ B. $\frac{3}{4}$ or $\frac{4}{5}$

   C. $\frac{7}{12}$ or $\frac{3}{5}$ D. $\frac{3}{8}$ or $\frac{4}{9}$

One way to find a common denominator for two fractions is to multiply the two denominators. Often, you can find a smaller common denominator. For example, $96 = 8 \times 12$. So 96 is a common denominator for $\frac{3}{8}$ and $\frac{5}{12}$. But 24 is also a multiple of 8 and 12. And 24 is easier to work with than 96. To compare $\frac{3}{8}$ and $\frac{5}{12}$, we write:

$$\frac{3 \times 3}{8 \times 3} = \frac{9}{24} \qquad \frac{5 \times 2}{12 \times 2} = \frac{10}{24}$$

Since $\frac{9}{24} < \frac{10}{24}$, we know that $\frac{3}{8} < \frac{5}{12}$.

3. Compare the following pairs of fractions. For each pair of fractions, find a common denominator that is smaller than the product of the denominators.

   A. $\frac{5}{12}$ $\frac{3}{9}$ B. $\frac{3}{10}$ $\frac{5}{15}$

   C. $\frac{8}{15}$ $\frac{5}{9}$ D. $\frac{5}{6}$ $\frac{7}{9}$

Student Guide - page 365 (Answers on p. 75)

TIMS Tip

Along with **Questions 1–3** in the *Student Guide,* there is some discussion of ways to find common denominators. For example, students are told that one way is to multiply both denominators together. But you may want students to think about ways to solve the problems without reading about specific methods first. You can write the questions on the board and then have students discuss the problems with their books closed.

Question 6 asks students what other methods they can use to compare fractions. Methods include using a calculator to convert the fraction to a decimal, comparing the fractions to benchmarks they know, and drawing pictures. Encourage students to choose efficient strategies for each problem. For example, in **Question 6F**, it is easier to compare $\frac{1}{9}$ and $\frac{7}{8}$ to the benchmark $\frac{1}{2}$ than to find a common denominator.

---

4. A survey said that $\frac{2}{3}$ of the households in Popperville read the *Daily Gazette* and that $\frac{3}{5}$ of the households read the *Daily News.* Which paper do more households read?

5. John helped his mother put shelves in his closet. He used a drill. He had 3 drill bits in sizes $\frac{3}{8}$ inch, $\frac{1}{2}$ inch, and $\frac{5}{16}$ inch. List the drill bit sizes in order, from smallest to largest.

6. Compare each pair of fractions. You may use any method you wish. Show the strategies you use.

   A. $\frac{6}{7}$ $\frac{1}{7}$ B. $\frac{5}{6}$ $\frac{3}{4}$ C. $\frac{2}{5}$ $\frac{2}{7}$

   D. $\frac{6}{11}$ $\frac{4}{9}$ E. $\frac{2}{3}$ $\frac{3}{5}$ F. $\frac{1}{9}$ $\frac{7}{8}$

 Homework

1. Find equivalent fractions:

   A. $\frac{3}{5} = \frac{?}{10}$ B. $\frac{5}{4} = \frac{15}{?}$

   C. $\frac{5}{9} = \frac{?}{36}$ D. $\frac{7}{10} = \frac{70}{?}$

2. Write each of the following pairs of fractions with a common denominator. Then compare the fractions. Use the symbols =, <, or > to write a number sentence involving each pair.

   A. $\frac{2}{3}$ $\frac{4}{6}$ B. $\frac{7}{12}$ $\frac{15}{24}$

   C. $\frac{3}{4}$ $\frac{8}{12}$ D. $\frac{4}{5}$ $\frac{20}{25}$

   E. $\frac{1}{5}$ $\frac{3}{8}$ F. $\frac{7}{8}$ $\frac{2}{3}$

   G. $\frac{3}{5}$ $\frac{6}{15}$ H. $\frac{3}{4}$ $\frac{5}{6}$

Student Guide - page 366 (Answers on p. 76)

Math Facts

DPP items M and P review the division facts for the 3s and the 9s through fact practice and finding factors of larger numbers.

Homework and Practice

- The questions in the Homework section of the *Comparing Fractions* Activity Pages provide more practice.

- Assign DPP items N–O. Item N provides practice with multiplication and division with whole and decimal numbers. Item O involves equivalent fractions.

- Assign Part 5 of the Home Practice that provides practice with computation.

Answers for Part 5 of the Home Practice are in the Answer Key at the end of this lesson and at the end of this unit.

Assessment

- Use DPP Task P to assess students' fluency with finding factors, prime numbers, and prime factorizations.

- Use the *Observational Assessment Record* to note students' abilities to find common denominators and compare fractions.

3. Compare each pair of fractions. You may use any method you wish. Show the strategies you use.

  A. $\frac{1}{4}$ $\frac{11}{12}$ B. $\frac{5}{6}$ $\frac{7}{8}$

  C. $\frac{3}{5}$ $\frac{3}{11}$ D. $\frac{1}{10}$ $\frac{10}{13}$

4. Compare the following. Write each pair of fractions with a common denominator that is smaller than the product of the denominators. For example, for Part A, find a denominator that is smaller than 12×8.

  A. $\frac{5}{12}$ $\frac{3}{8}$

  B. $\frac{5}{6}$ $\frac{3}{4}$

  C. $\frac{11}{18}$ $\frac{7}{12}$

5. John was hiking when he came to this sign on the trail. Which was closer, the overlook or the waterfall?

SCENIC OVERLOOK
2/5 miles

HARMONY FALLS
3/8 miles

6. John ordered a small pizza. It was cut into 6 equal pieces. His brother also ordered a small pizza from the same restaurant. It was cut into 4 equal pieces. John ate 4 of his 6 pieces, and his brother ate 3 of his 4 pieces. Who ate more pizza? Explain your answer.

Comparing Fractions   SG • Grade 5 • Unit 11 • Lesson 5   367

Student Guide - page 367 (Answers on p. 77)

Name _____ Date _____

PART 5 Practicing Computation

1. Solve the following problems using paper and pencil. Estimate to be sure your answers are reasonable. Explain your estimation strategies.

  A. $46 \times 23 =$ B. $372 \times 9 =$

2. Solve the following problems using a paper-and-pencil method. Express quotients as mixed numbers.

  A. $3850 \times 5 =$ B. $2076 \div 9 =$ C. $78 \times 19 =$

  D. $5945 + 6148 =$ E. $9035 - 2747 =$ F. $2703 \div 13 =$

NUMBER PATTERNS, PRIMES, AND FRACTIONS   DAB • Grade 5 • Unit 11 179

Discovery Assignment Book - page 179 (Answers on p. 77)

At a Glance

Math Facts and Daily Practice and Problems

DPP items M and P include a review of the division facts for the 3s and 9s. Item N practices computation with multiplication and division while item O involves finding equivalent fractions and comparing fractions.

Teaching the Activity

1. Briefly review equivalent fractions. Ask students to find three fractions that are equivalent to $\frac{2}{3}$ and to complete DPP item O.

2. Ask students to compare the following pairs of fractions and give reasons for their answers.
   $\frac{1}{12}$ and $\frac{9}{10}$
   $\frac{1}{3}$ and $\frac{2}{3}$
   $\frac{1}{2}$ and $\frac{1}{3}$
   $\frac{2}{3}$ and $\frac{3}{4}$

3. Read together the vignette on the *Comparing Fractions* Activity Pages in the *Student Guide* in which John and his mother compare $\frac{2}{3}$ and $\frac{3}{4}$.

4. Students answer *Questions 1–6* in the Discussion section.

Homework

1. Assign the questions in the Homework section.
2. Assign Part 5 of the Home Practice.

Assessment

1. Use DPP Task P as a quiz.
2. Use the *Observational Assessment Record* to note students' abilities to find common denominators and compare fractions.

Answer Key is on pages 75–77.

Notes:

Student Guide (p. 365)

1. A. $\frac{1}{2} = \frac{4}{8}$; since $\frac{4}{8} > \frac{3}{8}$, $\frac{1}{2} > \frac{3}{8}$

   B. $\frac{5}{6} = \frac{10}{12}$; since $\frac{10}{12} > \frac{7}{12}$, $\frac{5}{6} > \frac{7}{12}$

   C. $\frac{3}{4} = \frac{15}{20}$; since $\frac{17}{20} > \frac{15}{20}$, $\frac{17}{20} > \frac{3}{4}$

   D. $\frac{2}{3} = \frac{6}{9}$; since $\frac{6}{9} < \frac{7}{9}$, $\frac{2}{3} < \frac{7}{9}$

2. A. A common denominator for $\frac{4}{5}$ and $\frac{2}{3}$ is $5 \times 3 = 15$; $\frac{4}{5} = \frac{12}{15}$ and $\frac{2}{3} = \frac{10}{15}$. Since $\frac{12}{15} > \frac{10}{15}$, $\frac{4}{5}$ is larger than $\frac{2}{3}$.

   B. A common denominator for $\frac{3}{4}$ and $\frac{4}{5}$ is $4 \times 5 = 20$; $\frac{3}{4} = \frac{15}{20}$ and $\frac{4}{5} = \frac{16}{20}$. Since $\frac{15}{20} < \frac{16}{20}$, $\frac{3}{4}$ is less than $\frac{4}{5}$.

   C. A common denominator for $\frac{7}{12}$ and $\frac{3}{5}$ is $12 \times 5 = 60$; $\frac{7}{12} = \frac{35}{60}$ and $\frac{3}{5} = \frac{36}{60}$. Since $\frac{35}{60} < \frac{36}{60}$, $\frac{7}{12}$ is less than $\frac{3}{5}$.

   D. A common denominator for $\frac{3}{8}$ and $\frac{4}{9}$ is $8 \times 9 = 72$; $\frac{3}{8} = \frac{27}{72}$ and $\frac{4}{9} = \frac{32}{72}$. Since $\frac{27}{72} < \frac{32}{72}$, $\frac{3}{8}$ is less than $\frac{4}{9}$.

3. A. A common denominator for $\frac{5}{12}$ and $\frac{3}{9}$ is 36; $\frac{5}{12} = \frac{15}{36}$ and $\frac{3}{9} = \frac{12}{36}$. Since $\frac{15}{36} > \frac{12}{36}$, $\frac{5}{12}$ is larger than $\frac{3}{9}$.

   B. A common denominator for $\frac{3}{10}$ and $\frac{5}{15}$ is 30; $\frac{3}{10} = \frac{9}{30}$ and $\frac{5}{15} = \frac{10}{30}$. Since $\frac{9}{30} < \frac{10}{30}$, $\frac{3}{10}$ is less than $\frac{5}{15}$.

   C. A common denominator for $\frac{8}{15}$ and $\frac{5}{9}$ is 45; $\frac{8}{15} = \frac{24}{45}$ and $\frac{5}{9} = \frac{25}{45}$. Since $\frac{24}{45} < \frac{25}{45}$, $\frac{8}{15}$ is less than $\frac{5}{9}$.

   D. A common denominator for $\frac{5}{6}$ and $\frac{7}{9}$ is 18; $\frac{5}{6} = \frac{15}{18}$ and $\frac{7}{9} = \frac{14}{18}$. Since $\frac{15}{18} > \frac{14}{18}$, $\frac{5}{6}$ is larger than $\frac{7}{9}$.

Discuss

1. Write each pair of fractions with a common denominator. Then compare the fractions. Use the symbols < or >.

  A. $\frac{1}{2}$ $\frac{3}{8}$ **B.** $\frac{5}{6}$ $\frac{7}{12}$

  C. $\frac{17}{20}$ $\frac{3}{4}$ **D.** $\frac{2}{3}$ $\frac{7}{9}$

One way to find a common denominator for two fractions is to multiply both denominators together. For example, a common denominator for $\frac{2}{3}$ and $\frac{4}{5}$ is 15. Since $3 \times 5 = 15$, we know that 15 is a multiple of both 3 and 5.

2. Which is larger? To answer, find common denominators and compare.

  A. $\frac{4}{5}$ or $\frac{2}{3}$ **B.** $\frac{3}{4}$ or $\frac{4}{5}$

  C. $\frac{7}{12}$ or $\frac{3}{5}$ **D.** $\frac{3}{8}$ or $\frac{4}{9}$

One way to find a common denominator for two fractions is to multiply the two denominators. Often, you can find a smaller common denominator. For example, $96 = 8 \times 12$. So 96 is a common denominator for $\frac{3}{8}$ and $\frac{5}{12}$. But 24 is also a multiple of 8 and 12. And 24 is easier to work with than 96. To compare $\frac{3}{8}$ and $\frac{5}{12}$, we write:

$$\frac{3 \times 3}{8 \times 3} = \frac{9}{24} \qquad \frac{5 \times 2}{12 \times 2} = \frac{10}{24}$$

Since $\frac{9}{24} < \frac{10}{24}$, we know that $\frac{3}{8} < \frac{5}{12}$.

3. Compare the following pairs of fractions. For each pair of fractions, find a common denominator that is smaller than the product of the denominators.

  A. $\frac{5}{12}$ $\frac{3}{9}$ **B.** $\frac{3}{10}$ $\frac{5}{15}$

  C. $\frac{8}{15}$ $\frac{5}{9}$ **D.** $\frac{5}{6}$ $\frac{7}{9}$

Comparing Fractions   SG • Grade 5 • Unit 11 • Lesson 5   **365**

Student Guide - page 365

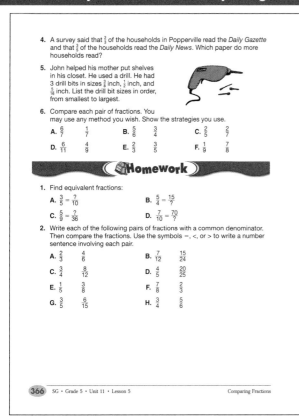

Student Guide - page 366

Student Guide (p. 366)

4. Since $\frac{2}{3} = \frac{10}{15}$ and $\frac{3}{5} = \frac{9}{15}$ and $\frac{10}{15} > \frac{9}{15}$, then $\frac{2}{3}$ is larger than $\frac{3}{5}$. Therefore, *Daily Gazette* has more subscribers.

5. $\frac{5}{16} < \frac{3}{8} < \frac{1}{2}$

6. Strategies will vary.

A. $\frac{6}{7} > \frac{1}{7}$

B. $\frac{5}{6} > \frac{3}{4}$

C. $\frac{2}{5} > \frac{2}{7}$

D. $\frac{6}{11} > \frac{4}{9}$

E. $\frac{2}{3} > \frac{3}{5}$

F. $\frac{1}{9} < \frac{7}{8}$*

Homework

1. **A.** $\frac{3}{5} = \frac{6}{10}$

   B. $\frac{5}{4} = \frac{15}{12}$

   C. $\frac{5}{9} = \frac{20}{36}$

   D. $\frac{7}{10} = \frac{70}{100}$

2. **A.** A common denominator is 6; $\frac{2}{3} = \frac{4}{6}$

   B. A common denominator is 24; $\frac{7}{12} = \frac{14}{24}$; $\frac{7}{12} < \frac{15}{24}$

   C. A common denominator is 12; $\frac{3}{4} = \frac{9}{12}$; $\frac{3}{4} > \frac{8}{12}$

   D. A common denominator is 25; $\frac{4}{5} = \frac{20}{25}$

   E. A common denominator is 40; $\frac{1}{5} = \frac{8}{40}$ and $\frac{3}{8} = \frac{15}{40}$ so $\frac{1}{5} < \frac{3}{8}$

   F. A common denominator is 24; $\frac{7}{8} = \frac{21}{24}$ and $\frac{2}{3} = \frac{16}{24}$ so $\frac{7}{8} > \frac{2}{3}$

   G. A common denominator is 15; $\frac{3}{5} = \frac{9}{15}$; $\frac{3}{5} > \frac{6}{15}$

   H. A common denominator is 24; $\frac{3}{4} = \frac{18}{24}$ and $\frac{5}{6} = \frac{20}{24}$ so $\frac{3}{4} < \frac{5}{6}$

*Answers and/or discussion are included in the Lesson Guide.

Student Guide (p. 367)

3. **A.** $\frac{1}{4} < \frac{11}{12}$

 B. $\frac{5}{6} < \frac{7}{8}$

 C. $\frac{3}{5} > \frac{3}{11}$

 D. $\frac{1}{10} < \frac{10}{13}$

4. **A.** A common denominator is 24; $\frac{5}{12} = \frac{10}{24}$ and $\frac{3}{8} = \frac{9}{24}$; $\frac{5}{12} > \frac{3}{8}$

 B. A common denominator is 12; $\frac{5}{6} = \frac{10}{12}$ and $\frac{3}{4} = \frac{9}{12}$; $\frac{5}{6} > \frac{3}{4}$

 C. A common denominator is 36; $\frac{11}{18} = \frac{22}{36}$ and $\frac{7}{12} = \frac{21}{36}$; $\frac{11}{18} > \frac{7}{12}$

5. A common denominator for $\frac{2}{5}$ and $\frac{3}{8}$ is 40; $\frac{2}{5} = \frac{16}{40}$ and $\frac{3}{8} = \frac{15}{40}$. Since $\frac{2}{5} > \frac{3}{8}$, the waterfall is closer.

6. John ate $\frac{4}{6}$ pizza and his brother ate $\frac{3}{4}$ pizza. A common denominator for $\frac{4}{6}$ and $\frac{3}{4}$ is 12; $\frac{4}{6} = \frac{8}{12}$ and $\frac{3}{4} = \frac{9}{12}$. Since $\frac{8}{12} < \frac{9}{12}$, John's brother ate more pizza.

Discovery Assignment Book (p. 179)

Home Practice*

Part 5. Practicing Computation

1. Estimation strategies will vary.

 A. 1058; $50 \times 20 = 1000$

 B. 3348. The answer will be less than 372×10 or 3720.

2. **A.** 19,250

 B. $230\frac{6}{9} = 230\frac{2}{3}$

 C. 1482

 D. 12,093

 E. 6288

 F. $207\frac{12}{13}$

Student Guide - page 367

Discovery Assignment Book - page 179

*Answers for all the Home Practice in the *Discovery Assignment Book* are at the end of the unit.

Lesson 6

Reducing Fractions

Lesson Overview

Estimated Class Sessions
1-2

Students use common factors to reduce fractions to lowest terms. They add and subtract fractions after finding common denominators, and they solve division problems whose quotients are mixed numbers. Then they express their answers in lowest terms.

Key Content

- Reducing fractions to lowest terms.
- Finding common denominators.
- Adding and subtracting fractions using common denominators.
- Expressing a quotient as a mixed number.

Key Vocabulary

- lowest terms
- reducing a fraction

Math Facts

DPP item Q reviews the division facts for the 3s and 9s.

Homework

1. Assign the problems in the Homework section of the *Reducing Fractions* Activity Pages.
2. Assign Parts 4 and 6 of the Home Practice.

Assessment

Students complete the *Skills Check-Up* Assessment Page.

Curriculum Sequence

Before This Unit

In Unit 5 Lessons 6 and 7, students added and subtracted fractions using rectangles on dot paper as a model. At that time they did not reduce their answers to lowest terms.

After This Unit

In Unit 12 students will add mixed numbers and multiply fractions.

Materials List

Supplies and Copies

Student	Teacher
Supplies for Each Student	**Supplies**
Copies • 1 copy of *Skills Check-Up* per student (*Unit Resource Guide* Page 84)	**Copies/Transparencies**

All blackline masters including assessment, transparency, and DPP masters are also on the Teacher Resource CD.

Student Books

Number Lines for Fractohoppers (*Student Guide* Page 82), optional
Reducing Fractions (*Student Guide* Pages 368–372)

Daily Practice and Problems and Home Practice

DPP items Q–R (*Unit Resource Guide* Pages 19–20)
Home Practice Parts 4 & 6 (*Discovery Assignment Book* Pages 178 & 180)

Note: Classrooms whose pacing differs significantly from the suggested pacing of the units should use the Math Facts Calendar in Section 4 of the *Facts Resource Guide* to ensure students receive the complete math facts program.

Daily Practice and Problems

Suggestions for using the DPPs are on page 82.

Q. Bit: Division Fact Practice IV
(URG p. 19)

A. $630 \div n = 7$

B. $n \div 300 = 7$

C. $5400 \div n = 90$

D. $27{,}000 \div 30 = n$

E. $8100 \div 900 = n$

F. $1800 \div n = 600$

R. Task: More Fractions
(URG p. 20)

1. Rewrite each fraction as a mixed number. Write all fractions in lowest terms.

A. $\frac{78}{8}$

B. $\frac{58}{12}$

C. $\frac{69}{15}$

2. Solve the following. Reduce your answers to lowest terms. Estimate to be sure your answers are reasonable.

A. $\frac{5}{18} + \frac{1}{6} =$

B. $\frac{4}{5} - \frac{3}{10} =$

C. $\frac{1}{2} - \frac{1}{30} =$

Teaching the Activity

Write the fraction $\frac{3}{6}$ on the board and ask students to:

- *Find a common factor of the numerator and denominator.* (3)

- *Divide both the numerator and the denominator by this factor.*

$$\frac{3}{6} = \frac{3 \div 3}{6 \div 3} = \frac{1}{2}$$

Students will probably recognize that $\frac{1}{2}$ is equivalent to $\frac{3}{6}$. If they do not, refer students to the Number Lines for Fractohoppers chart on page 82 in the *Student Guide* or have students multiply to get the original fraction back. You can try a few more fractions, such as $\frac{6}{8}$, $\frac{4}{6}$, and $\frac{3}{9}$. In each case, help students to understand that dividing a fraction's numerator and denominator by the same number results in a fraction equivalent to the first.

Next, students read the *Reducing Fractions* Activity Pages in the *Student Guide*. The pages introduce the word "reduce," and they discuss reducing fractions to lowest terms. Work on the questions in the discussion section. Ask students to share their solutions.

Reducing Fractions

"I know that multiplying the numerator and denominator of a fraction by the same number gives me a fraction that is equivalent to the first," Jackie said. "I remember that the rule is the same for division as for multiplication: dividing both the numerator and denominator by the same number gives a fraction that is equivalent to the first."

"Show me an example," said Mr. Moreno. "Try $\frac{4}{8}$."

"Okay," said Jackie. "I can divide both 4 and 8 by 4." She wrote:

$$\frac{4}{8} = \frac{4 \div 4}{8 \div 4} = \frac{1}{2}$$

"I remember that $\frac{4}{8}$ and $\frac{1}{2}$ are equivalent. We showed that before with pattern blocks. Dividing the numerator and denominator of $\frac{4}{8}$ by 4 gave me an equivalent fraction, $\frac{1}{2}$."

"You're right, Jackie, we can multiply the numerator and denominator of $\frac{1}{2}$ by 4 and get $\frac{4}{8}$ back," said Mr. Moreno.

$$\frac{1}{2} \times \frac{4}{4} = \frac{4}{8}$$

"Let's try some more. How about $\frac{12}{30}$?"

Jackie wrote:

$$\frac{12}{30} = \frac{12 \div 3}{30 \div 3} = \frac{4}{10}$$

"So $\frac{12}{30}$ is equivalent to $\frac{4}{10}$," she decided.

368 SG • Grade 5 • Unit 11 • Lesson 6 Reducing Fractions

Student Guide - page 368

Student Guide - page 369

Renaming a fraction with another fraction that has a smaller denominator is called **reducing** the fraction. To be able to reduce a fraction, the numerator and denominator need to have a common factor. In the example, Jackie divided 12 and 30 by their common factor, 3. Can she divide again? That is, can she find another common factor of the numerator and denominator and use it to reduce $\frac{4}{10}$?

The numerator and denominator of $\frac{4}{10}$ have the common factor 2. Divide the numerator and denominator by 2.

$$\frac{4}{10} = \frac{4 \div 2}{10 \div 2} = \frac{2}{5}$$

So $\frac{4}{10}$ is equivalent to $\frac{2}{5}$. When there are no other common factors other than 1, the fraction cannot be reduced anymore. We say it is in **lowest terms.** Reducing $\frac{12}{30}$ to lowest terms gives $\frac{2}{5}$.

Here is another example. Write $\frac{30}{36}$ in lowest terms. To do this, we can begin by dividing 30 and 36 by 2.

$$\frac{30 \div 2}{36 \div 2} = \frac{15}{18}$$

This fraction is not in lowest terms, because 15 and 18 have the common factor 3. So we'll reduce $\frac{15}{18}$.

$$\frac{15 \div 3}{18 \div 3} = \frac{5}{6}$$

Since 5 and 6 have no common factors other than one, $\frac{5}{6}$ is in lowest terms.

Discuss

1. Reduce the following fractions to lowest terms. If the fraction is already in lowest terms, say so.
   A. $\frac{12}{16}$ B. $\frac{20}{45}$ C. $\frac{15}{45}$
   D. $\frac{48}{60}$ E. $\frac{9}{26}$ F. $\frac{75}{100}$

2. Can you think of another way to reduce $\frac{30}{36}$ instead of dividing first by 2? If so, how?

3. Solve the following. Reduce your answers to lowest terms.
   A. $\frac{2}{15} + \frac{7}{15} =$ B. $\frac{11}{12} - \frac{5}{12} =$ C. $\frac{7}{16} + \frac{5}{16} =$

Student Guide - page 369 (Answers on p. 85)

Student Guide - page 370

4. Solve the following. Reduce your answers to lowest terms.
   A. $\frac{1}{4} + \frac{2}{3} =$
   B. $\frac{5}{12} + \frac{1}{3} =$
   C. $\frac{4}{5} - \frac{3}{10} =$

5. Jenny buys material to make doll clothes. She needs $\frac{1}{4}$ yard for the pants and $\frac{1}{3}$ yard for the shirts. How many yards does she need in all?

6. When Peter's family went camping, they brought a gallon of fuel to use in their camp stove and lantern. The stove held $\frac{1}{3}$ gallon of fuel, and the lantern held $\frac{1}{4}$ gallon.
   A. How much of the gallon was left after they filled the stove and the lantern?
   B. After filling the stove and the lantern, did they have enough fuel left in the tank to fill the lantern a second time? Explain your answer.
   C. Did they have enough fuel left to fill both the stove and the lantern a second time? Explain your answer.

7. Divide. Write each quotient as a mixed number. Reduce all fractions to lowest terms.
   A. $219 \div 9 =$
   B. $5230 \div 8 =$
   C. $7728 \div 36 =$

8. A. How many hours are there in 1180 minutes? Express your answer as a mixed number. Reduce.
   B. How many feet are there in 188 inches? Express your answer as a mixed number. Reduce.

9. Rename each decimal as a fraction and reduce to lowest terms.
   A. 0.8   B. 0.45   C. 0.250

Student Guide - page 370 (Answers on p. 85)

Student Guide - page 371

Homework

1. Reduce the following fractions to lowest terms. If a fraction is already in lowest terms, say so.
   A. $\frac{4}{10}$ B. $\frac{8}{24}$
   C. $\frac{18}{48}$ D. $\frac{12}{36}$
   E. $\frac{16}{64}$ F. $\frac{27}{81}$
   G. $\frac{7}{15}$ H. $\frac{60}{100}$

2. Solve the following. Reduce your answers to lowest terms.
   A. $\frac{5}{8} - \frac{3}{8} =$ B. $\frac{11}{24} + \frac{5}{24} =$ C. $\frac{7}{20} - \frac{3}{20} =$

3. Solve the following. Reduce your answers to lowest terms.
   A. $\frac{1}{2} + \frac{3}{10} =$ B. $\frac{5}{6} - \frac{1}{3} =$ C. $\frac{4}{5} + \frac{1}{10} =$

4. Rename each decimal as a fraction and reduce to lowest terms.
   A. 0.15   B. 0.4   C. 0.375

5. Abby's mother is making her a costume for the skating show. She needs to buy $\frac{1}{4}$ yard of sequins to go around the wrists, $\frac{2}{3}$ yard of sequins to trim her cape, and $\frac{2}{3}$ yard of sequins to go around the waist. The sequins are expensive, so she does not want to buy any more than she needs. How many yards of sequins should she buy? Express your answer as a mixed number, then reduce.

Student Guide - page 371 (Answers on p. 86)

Student Guide - page 372

6. Tim's family went for a walk around the 1-mile nature loop. They first walked $\frac{1}{3}$ mile to the waterfall. They continued $\frac{1}{4}$ mile farther along the trail until they came to a picnic area. While they were having their picnic, it started to rain. They wanted to return to their car the shortest way. Was it shorter for them to return along the trail the way they had come, or to continue around the loop until they came back to the parking lot? Give reasons for your answer.

7. Here is a data table showing the number of minutes Danny practiced violin each day last week. How many hours did he practice in all? Express your answer as a mixed number, then reduce.

Day	Minutes Practiced
Sunday	30
Monday	25
Tuesday	45
Wednesday	40
Thursday	20
Friday	0
Saturday	40

8. Divide. Write each quotient as a mixed number. Reduce all fractions.
   A. $472 \div 6 =$
   B. $3894 \div 4 =$
   C. $6970 \div 15 =$

Student Guide - page 372 (Answers on p. 86)

Name _____ Date _____

PART 3 Using Exponents

1. Each of the three numbers below is written as a product of primes. Rewrite the prime factorizations using exponents.

   A. $180 = 2 \times 3 \times 5 \times 2 \times 3 =$ _____

   B. $2125 = 5 \times 17 \times 5 \times 5 =$ _____

   C. $17,820 = 11 \times 2 \times 3 \times 3 \times 5 \times 2 \times 3 \times 3 =$ _____

2. Write each of the following numbers as a product of its primes without exponents. Use factor trees. Then write the number as a product of its primes using exponents.

   A. 20   B. 48   C. 56

PART 4 Fractions

1. Reduce the following fractions to lowest terms.

   A. $\frac{14}{28}$ B. $\frac{24}{42}$ C. $\frac{60}{200}$ D. $\frac{27}{90}$ E. $\frac{57}{120}$

2. Solve the following. First, find common denominators and then add or subtract. Reduce your answers to lowest terms.

   A. $\frac{4}{5} - \frac{3}{10} =$ B. $\frac{2}{5} - \frac{1}{15} =$ C. $\frac{5}{6} + \frac{1}{24} =$

Discovery Assignment Book - page 178 (Answers on p. 87)

Name _____ Date _____

PART 6 The Band

Choose an appropriate method to solve each of the following problems. For some questions you may need to find an exact answer, while for others you may only need an estimate. For each question, you may choose to use paper and pencil, mental math, or a calculator. Use a separate sheet of paper to explain how you solved each problem.

1. The Krinkles, a pop rock band from Chicago, recently toured the United States. Their tour van can travel about 12 miles on 1 gallon of gas. They bought about 200 gallons of gas on their tour. About how many miles did they travel?

2. If gas costs $1.50 per gallon, how much did the Krinkles spend on gas during their tour?

3. The Krinkles tour lasted 20 days. Each day the Krinkles budgeted $20 per person for food and $45 per person for a motel room. There are 5 members in the band. What was the total amount of money the band budgeted to spend on food, motel rooms, and gas?

4. On average, 300 people came to each of their concerts. Tickets were $5.00 per person at every concert.

   A. If they performed each of the 20 days of the tour, about how many people saw the Krinkles on tour?

   B. About how much money did they collect?

   C. After paying for gas, motels, and food, about how much money was left to pay the band?

   D. About how much did each member make?

   E. About how much did each band member make each day?

Discovery Assignment Book - page 180 (Answers on p. 87)

Questions 3–4 involve adding and subtracting fractions and then reducing answers to lowest terms. Students sometimes believe they can add or subtract fractions by adding or subtracting the numerators and denominators. Be sure they understand that this is not correct. For example, adding numerators and denominators in the expression $\frac{1}{2} + \frac{1}{4}$ would lead to the incorrect answer $\frac{2}{6}$ or $\frac{1}{3}$. Students can check that the correct answer to $\frac{1}{2} + \frac{1}{4}$ is $\frac{3}{4}$, not $\frac{1}{3}$. Encourage students to look back at their answers to see if they are reasonable. One strategy is to think about their work with pattern blocks (or other models). A red trapezoid ($\frac{1}{2}$) together with a brown trapezoid ($\frac{1}{4}$) are larger than a blue rhombus. They should also see that the sum of $\frac{1}{2}$ and another number should be larger than $\frac{1}{2}$, not smaller.

Math Facts

DPP item Q reviews the division facts for the 3s and 9s using multiples of 10.

Homework and Practice

• The problems in the Homework section of the *Reducing Fractions* Activity Pages provide more practice.

• Assign DPP Task R that reviews mixed numbers, fractions, lowest terms, and addition and subtraction.

• Assign Parts 4 and 6 of the Home Practice.

Answers for Parts 4 and 6 of the Home Practice are in the Answer Key at the end of this lesson and at the end of this unit.

Assessment

The *Skills Check-Up* Assessment Page assesses skills developed in this unit.

Extension

Ask students to investigate whether adding the same number to the numerator and denominator of a fraction results in a fraction that is equivalent to the first. It does not. Ask them to give examples to support their conclusions.

Math Facts and Daily Practice and Problems

DPP item Q reviews the division facts for the 3s and 9s. Task R reviews fraction concepts.

Teaching the Activity

1. Remind students that dividing the numerator and denominator of a fraction by the same number results in a fraction equivalent to the first. Demonstrate this by working with fractions such as $\frac{3}{6}$, $\frac{6}{8}$, $\frac{4}{6}$, and $\frac{3}{9}$.
2. Students read together the *Reducing Fractions* Activity Pages in the *Student Guide* that discuss reducing fractions to lowest terms.
3. Students answer and discuss together **Questions 1–9** in the Discussion section of the *Reducing Fractions* Activity Pages.

Homework

1. Assign the problems in the Homework section of the *Reducing Fractions* Activity Pages.
2. Assign Parts 4 and 6 of the Home Practice.

Assessment

Students complete the *Skills Check-Up* Assessment Page.

Extension

Have students investigate if adding the same number to a fraction's numerator and denominator results in a fraction equivalent to the first.

Answer Key is on pages 85–88.

Notes:

Skills Check-Up

Answer the following questions. You may use the tools you use in your classroom.

1. List all the factors for each number:

   A. 54: _____

   B. 38: _____

2. Rename each number below as a product of its prime factors using exponents. Organize your work in a factor tree.

   A. 270   **B.** 147

3. Reduce each fraction to its lowest terms.

   A. $\frac{5}{20}$ **B.** $\frac{14}{35}$

4. Use addition or subtraction to complete each number sentence.

   A. $\frac{3}{4} + \frac{5}{12} =$ **B.** $\frac{11}{24} - \frac{3}{8} =$

5. Rename each decimal as a fraction and reduce to lowest terms.

   A. 0.6   **B.** 0.125

Student Guide (pp. 369–370)

1. **A.** $\frac{12}{16} = \frac{3}{4}$

   B. $\frac{20}{30} = \frac{2}{3}$

   C. $\frac{15}{45} = \frac{1}{3}$

   D. $\frac{48}{60} = \frac{4}{5}$

   E. $\frac{9}{26}$ cannot be reduced.

   F. $\frac{75}{100} = \frac{3}{4}$

2. $\frac{30}{36} = \frac{30 \div 6}{36 \div 6} = \frac{5}{6}$

3. **A.** $\frac{9}{15} = \frac{3}{5}$

   B. $\frac{6}{12} = \frac{1}{2}$

   C. $\frac{12}{16} = \frac{3}{4}$

4. **A.** $\frac{11}{12}$

   B. $\frac{9}{12} = \frac{3}{4}$

   C. $\frac{5}{10} = \frac{1}{2}$

5. $\frac{1}{6} + \frac{1}{3} = \frac{1}{6} + \frac{2}{6} = \frac{3}{6}$ or $\frac{1}{2}$ yard

6. **A.** The stove and the lantern together held $\frac{1}{3} + \frac{1}{4} = \frac{7}{12}$ gallon of fuel. So there is $\frac{12}{12} - \frac{7}{12} = \frac{5}{12}$ gallon of fuel left in the tank.

   B. Yes; the stove holds $\frac{1}{3} = \frac{4}{12}$ gallon of fuel. Since $\frac{4}{12} < \frac{5}{12}$, they have enough fuel to fill the stove a second time.

   C. No; to fill the stove and the lantern a second time they needed $\frac{7}{12}$ gallon of fuel. Since they only had $\frac{5}{12}$, they didn't have enough.

7. **A.** $24\frac{3}{9} = 24\frac{1}{3}$

   B. $653\frac{6}{8} = 653\frac{3}{4}$

   C. $214\frac{24}{36} = 214\frac{2}{3}$

8. **A.** $19\frac{40}{60} = 19\frac{2}{3}$

   B. $15\frac{8}{12} = 15\frac{2}{3}$

9. **A.** $\frac{4}{5}$

   B. $\frac{9}{20}$

   C. $\frac{1}{4}$

Renaming a fraction with another fraction that has a smaller denominator is called **reducing** the fraction. To be able to reduce a fraction, the numerator and denominator need to have a common factor. In the example, Jackie divided 12 and 30 by their common factor, 3. Can she divide again? That is, can she find another common factor of the numerator and denominator and use it to reduce $\frac{4}{10}$?

The numerator and denominator of $\frac{4}{10}$ have the common factor 2. Divide the numerator and denominator by 2.

$$\frac{4}{10} = \frac{4 \div 2}{10 \div 2} = \frac{2}{5}$$

So $\frac{4}{10}$ is equivalent to $\frac{2}{5}$. When there are no other common factors other than 1, the fraction cannot be reduced anymore. We say it is in **lowest terms**. Reducing $\frac{12}{30}$ to lowest terms gives $\frac{2}{5}$.

Here is another example. Write $\frac{30}{36}$ in lowest terms. To do this, we can begin by dividing 30 and 36 by 2.

$$\frac{30 \div 2}{36 \div 2} = \frac{15}{18}$$

This fraction is not in lowest terms, because 15 and 18 have the common factor 3. So we'll reduce $\frac{15}{18}$.

$$\frac{15 \div 3}{18 \div 3} = \frac{5}{6}$$

Since 5 and 6 have no common factors other than one, $\frac{5}{6}$ is in lowest terms.

Discuss

1. Reduce the following fractions to lowest terms. If the fraction is already in lowest terms, say so.

   A. $\frac{12}{16}$ **B.** $\frac{20}{30}$ **C.** $\frac{15}{45}$

   D. $\frac{48}{60}$ **E.** $\frac{9}{26}$ **F.** $\frac{75}{100}$

2. Can you think of another way to reduce $\frac{30}{36}$ instead of dividing first by 2? If so, how?

3. Solve the following. Reduce your answers to lowest terms.

   A. $\frac{2}{15} + \frac{7}{15} =$ **B.** $\frac{11}{12} - \frac{5}{12} =$ **C.** $\frac{7}{16} + \frac{5}{16} =$

Reducing Fractions   SG • Grade 5 • Unit 11 • Lesson 6   **369**

Student Guide - page 369

---

4. Solve the following. Reduce your answers to lowest terms.

   A. $\frac{1}{4} + \frac{2}{3} =$

   B. $\frac{5}{12} + \frac{1}{3} =$

   C. $\frac{4}{5} - \frac{3}{10} =$

5. Jenny buys material to make doll clothes. She needs $\frac{1}{6}$ yard for the pants and $\frac{1}{3}$ yard for the shirts. How many yards does she need in all?

6. When Peter's family went camping, they brought a gallon of fuel to use in their camp stove and lantern. The stove held $\frac{1}{3}$ gallon of fuel, and the lantern held $\frac{1}{4}$ gallon.

   A. How much of the gallon was left after they filled the stove and the lantern?

   B. After filling the stove and the lantern, did they have enough fuel left in the tank to fill the lantern a second time? Explain your answer.

   C. Did they have enough fuel left to fill both the stove and the lantern a second time? Explain your answer.

7. Divide. Write each quotient as a mixed number. Reduce all fractions to lowest terms.

   A. $219 \div 9 =$

   B. $5230 \div 8 =$

   C. $7728 \div 36 =$

8. **A.** How many hours are there in 1180 minutes? Express your answer as a mixed number. Reduce.

   B. How many feet are there in 188 inches? Express your answer as a mixed number. Reduce.

9. Rename each decimal as a fraction and reduce to lowest terms.

   A. 0.8   **B.** 0.45   **C.** 0.250

370   SG • Grade 5 • Unit 11 • Lesson 6   Reducing Fractions

Student Guide - page 370

Homework

1. Reduce the following fractions to lowest terms. If a fraction is already in lowest terms, say so.

   A. $\frac{4}{10}$ B. $\frac{8}{24}$

   C. $\frac{18}{48}$ D. $\frac{12}{36}$

   E. $\frac{16}{64}$ F. $\frac{27}{81}$

   G. $\frac{7}{15}$ H. $\frac{60}{100}$

2. Solve the following. Reduce your answers to lowest terms.

   A. $\frac{5}{8} - \frac{3}{8} =$ B. $\frac{11}{24} + \frac{5}{24} =$ C. $\frac{7}{20} - \frac{3}{20} =$

3. Solve the following. Reduce your answers to lowest terms.

   A. $\frac{1}{2} + \frac{3}{10} =$ B. $\frac{5}{6} - \frac{1}{3} =$ C. $\frac{4}{5} + \frac{1}{10} =$

4. Rename each decimal as a fraction and reduce to lowest terms.

   A. 0.15   B. 0.4   C. 0.375

5. Abby's mother is making her a costume for the skating show. She needs to buy $\frac{1}{4}$ yard of sequins to go around the wrists, $\frac{5}{6}$ yard of sequins to trim her cape, and $\frac{2}{3}$ yard of sequins to go around the waist. The sequins are expensive, so she does not want to buy any more than she needs. How many yards of sequins should she buy? Express your answer as a mixed number, then reduce.

Student Guide - page 371

6. Tim's family went for a walk around the 1-mile nature loop. They first walked $\frac{1}{3}$ mile to the waterfall. They continued $\frac{1}{4}$ mile farther along the trail until they came to a picnic area. While they were having their picnic, it started to rain. They wanted to return to their car the shortest way. Was it shorter for them to return along the trail the way they had come, or to continue around the loop until they came back to the parking lot? Give reasons for your answer.

7. Here is a data table showing the number of minutes Danny practiced violin each day last week. How many hours did he practice in all? Express your answer as a mixed number, then reduce.

Day	Minutes Practiced
Sunday	30
Monday	25
Tuesday	45
Wednesday	40
Thursday	20
Friday	0
Saturday	40

8. Divide. Write each quotient as a mixed number. Reduce all fractions.

   A. 472 ÷ 6 =
   B. 3894 ÷ 4 =
   C. 6970 ÷ 15 =

Student Guide - page 372

Student Guide (pp. 371–372)

Homework

1. **A.** $\frac{4}{10} = \frac{2}{5}$

   B. $\frac{8}{24} = \frac{1}{3}$

   C. $\frac{18}{48} = \frac{3}{8}$

   D. $\frac{12}{36} = \frac{1}{3}$

   E. $\frac{16}{64} = \frac{1}{4}$

   F. $\frac{27}{81} = \frac{1}{3}$

   G. cannot be reduced

   H. $\frac{60}{100} = \frac{3}{5}$

2. **A.** $\frac{2}{8} = \frac{1}{4}$

   B. $\frac{16}{24} = \frac{2}{3}$

   C. $\frac{4}{20} = \frac{1}{5}$

3. **A.** $\frac{8}{10} = \frac{4}{5}$

   B. $\frac{3}{6} = \frac{1}{2}$

   C. $\frac{9}{10}$

4. **A.** $\frac{3}{20}$

   B. $\frac{2}{5}$

   C. $\frac{3}{8}$

5. $\frac{1}{4} + \frac{5}{6} + \frac{2}{3} = \frac{3}{12} + \frac{10}{12} + \frac{8}{12} = \frac{21}{12} = 1\frac{9}{12} = 1\frac{3}{4}$ yards

6. They should continue around the loop. They walked a total distance of $\frac{1}{3} + \frac{1}{4} = \frac{7}{12}$ mile. There is $\frac{12}{12} - \frac{7}{12} = \frac{5}{12}$ mile left to go around the loop to get to the parking lot. Since $\frac{5}{12}$ is smaller than $\frac{7}{12}$ it will be shorter for them to continue around the loop.

7. $3\frac{20}{60} = 3\frac{1}{3}$ hours

8. **A.** $78\frac{4}{6} = 78\frac{2}{3}$

   B. $973\frac{2}{4} = 973\frac{1}{2}$

   C. $464\frac{10}{15} = 464\frac{2}{3}$

Discovery Assignment Book (p. 178)

Home Practice*

Part 4. Fractions

1. A. $\frac{1}{2}$

    B. $\frac{4}{7}$

    C. $\frac{3}{10}$

    D. $\frac{3}{10}$

    E. $\frac{19}{40}$

2. A. $\frac{5}{10} = \frac{1}{2}$

    B. $\frac{5}{15} = \frac{1}{3}$

    C. $\frac{21}{24} = \frac{7}{8}$

Name _____ Date _____

PART 3 Using Exponents

1. Each of the three numbers below is written as a product of primes. Rewrite the prime factorizations using exponents.

   A. $180 = 2 \times 3 \times 5 \times 2 \times 3 =$ _____

   B. $2125 = 5 \times 17 \times 5 \times 5 =$ _____

   C. $17,820 = 11 \times 2 \times 3 \times 3 \times 5 \times 2 \times 3 \times 3 =$ _____

2. Write each of the following numbers as a product of its primes without exponents. Use factor trees. Then write the number as a product of its primes using exponents.

   A. 20   B. 48   C. 56

PART 4 Fractions

1. Reduce the following fractions to lowest terms.

   A. $\frac{14}{28}$ B. $\frac{24}{42}$ C. $\frac{60}{200}$ D. $\frac{27}{90}$ E. $\frac{57}{120}$

2. Solve the following. First, find common denominators and then add or subtract. Reduce your answers to lowest terms.

   A. $\frac{4}{5} - \frac{3}{10} =$ B. $\frac{2}{5} - \frac{1}{15} =$ C. $\frac{5}{6} + \frac{1}{24} =$

178 DAB • Grade 5 • Unit 11   NUMBER PATTERNS, PRIMES, AND FRACTIONS

Discovery Assignment Book - page 178

Discovery Assignment Book (p. 180)

Part 6. The Band

1. About 2400 miles

2. $300

3. $6500 + $300 = $6800

4. A. 6000 people

    B. $30,000

    C. $30,000 − $6800 = $23,200

    D. $4640

    E. $232

Name _____ Date _____

PART 6 The Band

Choose an appropriate method to solve each of the following problems. For some questions you may need to find an exact answer, while for others you may only need an estimate. For each question, you may choose to use paper and pencil, mental math, or a calculator. Use a separate sheet of paper to explain how you solved each problem.

1. The Krinkles, a pop rock band from Chicago, recently toured the United States. Their tour van can travel about 12 miles on 1 gallon of gas. They bought about 200 gallons of gas on their tour. About how many miles did they travel?

2. If gas costs $1.50 per gallon, how much did the Krinkles spend on gas during their tour?

3. The Krinkles tour lasted 20 days. Each day the Krinkles budgeted $20 per person for food and $45 per person for a motel room. There are 5 members in the band. What was the total amount of money the band budgeted to spend on food, motel rooms, and gas?

4. On average, 300 people came to each of their concerts. Tickets were $5.00 per person at every concert.

   A. If they performed each of the 20 days of the tour, about how many people saw the Krinkles on tour?

   B. About how much money did they collect?

   C. After paying for gas, motels, and food, about how much money was left to pay the band?

   D. About how much did each member make?

   E. About how much did each band member make each day?

180 DAB • Grade 5 • Unit 11   NUMBER PATTERNS, PRIMES, AND FRACTIONS

Discovery Assignment Book - page 180

*Answers for all the Home Practice in the *Discovery Assignment Book* are at the end of the unit.

Name _____ Date _____

Skills Check-Up

Answer the following questions. You may use the tools you use in your classroom.

1. List all the factors for each number:

   A. 54: _____

   B. 38: _____

2. Rename each number below as a product of its prime factors using exponents. Organize your work in a factor tree.

   A. 270   B. 147

3. Reduce each fraction to its lowest terms.

   A. $\frac{5}{20}$ B. $\frac{14}{35}$

4. Use addition or subtraction to complete each number sentence.

   A. $\frac{3}{4} + \frac{5}{12} =$ B. $\frac{11}{24} - \frac{3}{8} =$

5. Rename each decimal as a fraction and reduce to lowest terms.

   A. 0.6   B. 0.125

Copyright © Kendall/Hunt Publishing Company

Unit Resource Guide - page 84

Unit Resource Guide (p. 84)

Skills Check-Up

1. **A.** 1, 2, 3, 6, 9, 18, 27, and 54

   B. 1, 2, 19, and 38

2. **A.** $2 \times 3^3 \times 5 = 270$

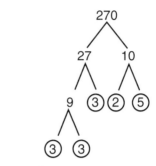

   B. $3 \times 7^2 = 147$

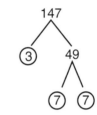

3. **A.** $\frac{1}{4}$

   B. $\frac{2}{5}$

4. **A.** $\frac{14}{12} = \frac{7}{6} = 1\frac{1}{6}$

   B. $\frac{2}{24} = \frac{1}{12}$

5. **A.** $\frac{6}{10} = \frac{3}{5}$

   B. $\frac{125}{1000} = \frac{1}{8}$

A Further Look at Patterns and Primes

Estimated Class Sessions

2

Lesson Overview

In this assessment activity, students use the Sieve of Eratosthenes to find the prime numbers from 1 to 100 on a *6-column 100 Chart*. Students identify and write about the resulting patterns. This activity assesses students' knowledge of primes and multiples as well as their communication skills.

Key Content

- Identifying and describing number patterns.
- Identifying prime numbers.
- Communicating mathematically.

Math Facts

DPP items S and U review math facts.

Homework

Assign some or all of the word problems in Lesson 8 as homework.

Assessment

1. Have students put their work for this activity in their collection folders for possible inclusion in their portfolios.
2. Use the *Observational Assessment Record* to note students' abilities to identify and describe number patterns. Transfer your observations to students' *Individual Assessment Record Sheets*.

Curriculum Sequence

Before This Unit

Students have described patterns and problem-solving strategies using the Student Rubrics as a guide throughout fifth grade. In particular, see *Stack Up* in Unit 2 Lesson 9, *Making Shapes* in Unit 6 Lesson 7, *Florence Kelley's Report* in Unit 8 Lesson 4, and *Grass Act* in Unit 9 Lesson 6.

Materials List

Supplies and Copies

Student	Teacher
Supplies for Each Student • 4 different-colored crayons	**Supplies**
Copies • 1 copy of *A Further Look at Patterns and Primes* per student (*Unit Resource Guide* Page 98) • 1 copy of *6-column 100 Chart* per student (*Unit Resource Guide* Page 99)	**Copies/Transparencies** • 1 copy of *TIMS Multidimensional Rubric* (*Teacher Implementation Guide,* Assessment section) • 1 transparency or poster of Student Rubric: *Telling,* optional (*Teacher Implementation Guide,* Assessment section)

All blackline masters including assessment, transparency, and DPP masters are also on the Teacher Resource CD.

Student Books
Student Rubric: *Telling* (*Student Guide* Appendix C and Inside Back Cover)

Daily Practice and Problems and Home Practice
DPP items S–V (*Unit Resource Guide* Pages 20–22)

Note: Classrooms whose pacing differs significantly from the suggested pacing of the units should use the Math Facts Calendar in Section 4 of the *Facts Resource Guide* to ensure students receive the complete math facts program.

Assessment Tools
TIMS *Multidimensional Rubric* (*Teacher Implementation Guide,* Assessment section)
Observational Assessment Record (*Unit Resource Guide* Pages 11–12)
Individual Assessment Record Sheet (*Teacher Implementation Guide,* Assessment section)

Daily Practice and Problems

Suggestions for using the DPPs are on page 96.

S. Bit: Practice: 3s and 9s (URG p. 20)

A. $30 \div 3 =$ B. $45 \div 5 =$
C. $90 \div 10 =$ D. $18 \div 6 =$
E. $24 \div 8 =$ F. $9 \div 3 =$
G. $54 \div 6 =$ H. $18 \div 2 =$
I. $81 \div 9 =$ J. $12 \div 3 =$
K. $63 \div 7 =$ L. $21 \div 7 =$
M. $15 \div 5 =$ N. $6 \div 3 =$
O. $27 \div 9 =$ P. $36 \div 4 =$
Q. $72 \div 8 =$

T. Task: Practice (URG p. 21)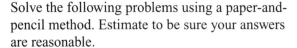

Solve the following problems using a paper-and-pencil method. Estimate to be sure your answers are reasonable.

1. A. $18 \times 65 =$
   B. $127 \times 62 =$
   C. $7641 \times 8 =$
2. A. $2309 \div 7 =$
   B. $2459 \div 12 =$
   C. $6608 \div 28 =$
3. Explain your estimation strategies for 1A and 2A.

U. Bit: Products of Primes (URG p. 21)

Solve the following in your head.

A. $2^2 \times 3^2 =$ B. $5^2 \times 2^2 =$
C. $2^3 \times 3 =$ D. $3^2 \times 7 =$

V. Challenge: Logic (URG p. 22)

Latisha, Jackie, Edward, and Carlos are planting trees for Arbor Day. Each will plant a different kind of tree. They are planting white pine, red bud, flowering crab, and oak trees. One of them is planting 20 trees while the others are planting 12, 13, and 14 trees. Use the following clues to find who is planting each kind of tree and how many they are planting.

Clues:

A. Latisha will plant more than the girl planting the flowering crab trees and the boy with the oak trees, but she will plant fewer trees than Carlos.

B. Jackie will plant fewer trees than Carlos and the girl planting the red bud trees, but she will plant more than the boy planting the oak trees.

This assessment is similar to the activity in Lesson 2; however, in this activity students sift for primes using a *6-column 100 Chart* instead of a traditional *100 Chart*. After completing the chart, they find several different patterns and write about the patterns they see.

Distribute *A Further Look at Patterns and Primes* and the *6-column 100 Chart* Assessment Pages from the *Unit Resource Guide* and read through the directions. Make sure students understand that they will circle the prime numbers and mark out multiples of the numbers 2, 3, 5, and 7 on a *6-column 100 Chart*. They should use a different-colored crayon to identify the multiples of each of these numbers. If a number is a multiple of more than one of these numbers, it should be marked with more than one color. For example, 6 is a multiple of both 2 and 3. If you shade all of the multiples of 2 yellow and draw a green, vertical line through all of the

multiples of 3, then the box containing the number 6 should be marked with both yellow and green (see Figure 11).

| 1NO | ② | ③ | 4 | 5 | 6 |

Figure 11: *Marking the multiples of 2 and 3*

While students should be able to complete this chart independently, you may have them work with a partner. Once a student completes the sifting process for the multiples of all four prime numbers, he or she is ready to look for and write about the patterns in the completed chart. See Figure 12.

Review the Student Rubric: *Telling* to help students understand your expectations for their work on the assessment. Tell them you will score their work based on this rubric. At this point, students should work independently to explain in writing the patterns they find.

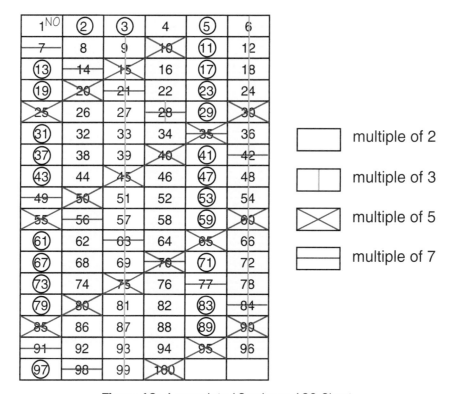

Figure 12: *A completed* 6-column 100 Chart

Some patterns that students might write about include:

- All the prime numbers, except for the numbers 2 and 3, are in the first and fifth columns.
- The prime numbers are all odd except for 2.
- All the multiples of 2 are in columns two, four, and six.
- All the multiples of 2 are even numbers.
- The multiples of 3 are in the third and sixth columns.
- Every other multiple of 3 is also a multiple of 2.
- The multiples of 5 form diagonals that begin at the right and go down.
- The multiples of 7 form diagonals that begin at the left and go down.
- Every other multiple of 5 is also a multiple of 2. These multiples end in 0.
- Every other multiple of 7 is also a multiple of 2.
- To find common factors, you can look for numbers that have the same colors. For example, 27 and 12 have 3 as a common factor because they both have the color for three in their box.

Once students finish writing, review their work and provide feedback so they can make revisions. Feedback should encourage students to clarify or expand on what they wrote. You can also direct students to look back at their *6-column 100 Chart* to find additional information or patterns.

Score students' work using the Telling Dimension of the *TIMS Multidimensional Rubric.* To help you assign scores, questions specific to this task are listed below:

Telling:

- Did the student find sufficient patterns to indicate he or she analyzed the chart completely and carefully?
- Did the student clearly describe each pattern that he or she found?
- Did the student support each pattern with examples from the chart?
- Did the student use terms like "prime number," "multiple," and "factor" correctly when describing the patterns?

Here are two samples of student work scored using the Telling Dimension.

TIMS Tip

Written feedback provides you with a permanent record of a student's progress toward effective communication. Your suggestions for clarification or expansion will help establish what a student can do independently and what a student can do with additional input or structure. If you give a student verbal feedback, make a note in your record so you can differentiate between what the student accomplished independently and what the student accomplished with additional input from you.

Student A

Student A completed the *6-column 100 Chart* correctly and wrote the following:

My 6-Column 100-Chart

Today, in the afternoon, our teacher gave us a chart of 6-columns 100 chart to find the multiples of 2,3,5, and 7. Here are a few patterns that we found. I found that the multiples of "2" are in columns 2, 4, 6th columns, all multiples of 2 are even. The number 2 is prime and even, It's the only even number that is prime.

All the multiples of 3 are in column 3 and 6th. The 3 has multiples of 2 for example 6,12,18..., also it shares multiples of 5 and 7 like in 5, 5, 15; 14. The 7, shares multiples with the #3 : 7,21,63,84,

The multiples of 5 end up in 5 or 0 and are in a diagonal. There are 4 diagonals of 5, they go in a diagonal from right to left, also every other multiple of 5 shares multiples of 2. First look for all the numbers with a "0" and that is also a multiple of 2: 10,20,30,40,50...

The seven goes in a diagonal from left to right, opposite of 5. Every other multiple of 7 end up in a even number like: 0,2,4,6,8 are multiples of 2. Finally, I had lots of fun finding patterns because it's like a challenge.

Student A scored a 3 on the Telling Dimension. His response is fairly complete and clear. He readily explains patterns for the multiples of 2, 3, 5, and 7. However, he does not give much information about the primes in the chart nor does he use the terms "composite" or "factor" as the directions ask. He does give examples to support his discussion of the multiples. For example, he describes the diagonals formed by the multiples of 5 and says, ". . . also every other multiple of 5 shares multiples of 2. First look for all the numbers with a '0' and that is also a multiple of 2: 10, 20, 30, 40, 50. . . ." However, in one paragraph he incorrectly says, ". . . it (3) shares multiples of 5 and 7 like in 5, 5, 15; 14." He used the terms "prime," "multiple," and "even" with only minor errors.

Telling	Level 4	Level 3	Level 2	Level 1
Includes response with an explanation and/or description which is…	Complete and clear	Fairly complete and clear	Perhaps ambiguous or unclear	Totally unclear or irrelevant
Presents supporting arguments which are…	Strong and sound	Logically sound, but may contain minor gaps	Incomplete or logically unsound	Not present
Uses pictures, symbols, tables, and graphs which are…	Correct and clearly relevant	Present with minor errors or some-what irrelevant	Present with errors and/or irrelevant	Not present or completely inappropriate
Uses terminology…	Clearly and precisely	With minor errors	With major errors	Not at all

Figure 13: *Student A's work and scores on the Telling Rubric*

Student B

Student B also completed the chart correctly.
She wrote the following:

6-column 100 chart

today in the afternoon our teacher gave us a 6-column 100 chart, and another paper that had steps for doing the chart. The first step is to cross the first number of the chart. Then it told me to circle the number two because the number two is prime. It told me to color over all the multiples of two. The prime numbers that I circled were 2,3,5,7. The patterns that I found for the number two is that the end of the multiples of two are numbers that are even, and that the multiples of two are multiples of other numbers. The patterns that I found in the prime number 3 is that multiples of three are the multiples of other numbers. The other pattern that I found for all the prime numbers, and the other num is that you are doubling the number. I know that the number 2 is the first prime number. The patterns that I found for the number five are that all multiples of five end with zero, and with 5. I know that other numbers have multiples of even if they are odd or they are even, it doesn't matter and I know that five has 4 diagonal and it's intersecting with the other prime numbers. the patterns that I see for the prime number seven are that it has multiples of the other numbers like 3 of like 5.

Finally, I think 6-column 100 chart was a little difficult to do for the people that don't know what the prime numbers are,

Telling	Level 4	Level 3	Level 2	Level 1
Includes response with an explanation and/or description which is…	Complete and clear	Fairly complete and clear	Perhaps ambiguous or unclear	Totally unclear or irrelevant
Presents supporting arguments which are…	Strong and sound	Logically sound, but may contain minor gaps	Incomplete or logically unsound	Not present
Uses pictures, symbols, tables, and graphs which are…	Correct and clearly relevant	Present with minor errors or somewhat irrelevant	Present with errors and/or irrelevant	Not present or completely inappropriate
Uses terminology…	Clearly and precisely	With minor errors	With major errors	Not at all

Figure 14: *Student B's work and scores on the* Telling *Rubric*

Student B scored a 2 on the Telling Dimension. The beginning of her discussion is a fairly clear explanation of the process. However, much of her writing is confused and often includes the incorrect use of terms. For example, she says, "I know that other numbers have multiples of even if they are odd or they are even, it doesn't matter, ..."

Math Facts

DPP item S provides practice with the division facts for the 3s and 9s. Item U provides practice with facts using exponents.

Homework and Practice

- Assign the word problems in Lesson 8 for homework. Encourage students to describe their solution strategies.
- Assign DPP items S–V. Task T provides practice with multiplication and division using paper-and-pencil methods.

Assessment

- Ask students to put their work for this activity in their collection folders for possible inclusion in their portfolios. Review portfolios. Students can compare their writing for this lesson to the writing they did for the assessment lessons *Stack Up* in Unit 2 Lesson 9 and *Florence Kelley's Report* in Unit 8 Lesson 4.
- Use the *Observational Assessment Record* to note students' abilities to identify and describe number patterns. Transfer your observations to students' *Individual Assessment Record Sheets*.

Extension

Item V is a challenging logic problem.

At a Glance

Math Facts and Daily Practice and Problems

DPP items S and U review math facts. Task T provides practice with computation with multiplication and division. Challenge V is a logic puzzle.

Teaching the Activity

1. Distribute *A Further Look at Patterns and Primes* Assessment Page and a *6-column 100 Chart* to each student. These pages are in the *Unit Resource Guide.*
2. Make sure each student has four different-colored crayons and a pencil.
3. Read the directions and check for student understanding.
4. Students complete the *6-column 100 Chart* either independently or with a partner.
5. Review the *Telling* rubric with students.
6. Students write about the patterns they find in their charts.
7. Review written work and provide feedback to students for revision.
8. After work is revised, score student work using the Telling Dimension of the *TIMS Multidimensional Rubric.*
9. Students place their work in their collection folders and review their portfolios. They compare their work to similar assessments.

Homework

Assign some or all of the word problems in Lesson 8 as homework.

Assessment

1. Have students put their work for this activity in their collection folders for possible inclusion in their portfolios.
2. Use the *Observational Assessment Record* to note students' abilities to identify and describe number patterns. Transfer your observations to students' *Individual Assessment Record Sheets.*

Extension

Assign DPP item V.

Answer Key is on page 100.

Notes:

A Further Look at Patterns and Primes

A Different Sieve

You will need four different-colored crayons to complete this activity.

Sift for primes using a *6-column 100 Chart.* Mark out all the multiples of 2, 3, 5, and 7 following the directions below. Circle all the primes.

- Since 1 is neither prime nor composite, begin by writing "No" on the number 1.
- Since 2 is a prime, use one color to circle the number 2. To mark out all the multiples of 2, use this color to lightly shade all the multiples of 2. (*Hint:* Use a light color such as yellow.)

    multiple of 2

- Using a different color, circle the number 3. Use this color to draw a vertical line (|) through all the multiples of 3.

    multiple of 3

- Using a third color, circle the number 5. Use this color to write an x on all of the multiples of 5.

    multiple of 5

- Using a fourth color, circle the number 7. Use this color to draw a horizontal line (–) through all the multiples of 7.

    multiple of 7

- Any number on the chart that is not marked out with one of the four colors is a prime number. Circle all the primes.

Look carefully at your chart. Write about all the patterns you see. Use words like prime, composite, factor, and multiple to explain your patterns. Use the Student Rubric: *Telling* to guide you as you write. You can find the *Telling* Rubric on the inside back cover of your *Student Guide.*

Note: If a number is a multiple of more than one number, it will be marked with more than one color.

6-column 100 Chart

1	2	3	4	5	6
7	8	9	10	11	12
13	14	15	16	17	18
19	20	21	22	23	24
25	26	27	28	29	30
31	32	33	34	35	36
37	38	39	40	41	42
43	44	45	46	47	48
49	50	51	52	53	54
55	56	57	58	59	60
61	62	63	64	65	66
67	68	69	70	71	72
73	74	75	76	77	78
79	80	81	82	83	84
85	86	87	88	89	90
91	92	93	94	95	96
97	98	99	100		

Unit Resource Guide (p. 98)

A Further Look at Patterns and Primes

See Figure 12 in Lesson Guide 7. See the Lesson Guide for sample student work as well.*

Name _____ Date _____

A Further Look at
Patterns and Primes

A Different Sieve

You will need four different-colored crayons to complete this activity.

Sift for primes using a *6-column 100 Chart*. Mark out all the multiples of 2, 3, 5, and 7 following the directions below. Circle all the primes.

- Since 1 is neither prime nor composite, begin by writing "No" on the number 1.
- Since 2 is a prime, use one color to circle the number 2. To mark out all the multiples of 2, use this color to lightly shade all the multiples of 2. (*Hint:* Use a light color such as yellow.)

  ▨ multiple of 2

- Using a different color, circle the number 3. Use this color to draw a vertical line (|) through all the multiples of 3.

  ▯ multiple of 3

- Using a third color, circle the number 5. Use this color to write an x on all of the multiples of 5.

  ⊠ multiple of 5

- Using a fourth color, circle the number 7. Use this color to draw a horizontal line (–) through all the multiples of 7.

  ▭ multiple of 7

- Any number on the chart that is not marked out with one of the four colors is a prime number. Circle all the primes.

Look carefully at your chart. Write about all the patterns you see. Use words like prime, composite, factor, and multiple to explain your patterns. Use the Student Rubric: *Telling* to guide you as you write. You can find the *Telling* Rubric on the inside back cover of your *Student Guide*.

Note: If a number is a multiple of more than one number, it will be marked with more than one color.

98   URG • Grade 5 • Unit 11 • Lesson 7   Assessment Blackline Master

Copyright © Kendall/Hunt Publishing Company

Unit Resource Guide - page 98

---

*Answers and/or discussion are included in the Lesson Guide.

From Factors to Fractions

Lesson Overview

Estimated Class Sessions

1

Students solve a variety of multistep word problems.

Key Content

- Solving multistep word problems.
- Communicating solutions orally and in writing.
- Choosing appropriate methods and tools to calculate (calculators, paper and pencil, or mental math).

Homework

Assign some or all of the problems for homework.

Materials List

Supplies and Copies

Student	Teacher
Supplies for Each Student • calculator	**Supplies**
Copies	**Copies/Transparencies**

All blackline masters including assessment, transparency, and DPP masters are also on the Teacher Resource CD.

Student Books

From Factors to Fractions (*Student Guide* Page 373)

From Factors to Fractions

Complete each of the following problems. Show how you found each solution.

1. Romesh and John were playing *Factor 40* after school. John made the first move. He chose to circle 29.

   A. Was this a good first move? Explain the reasons for your answer.

   B. Was there a better first move? Explain your thinking.

2. Arti's family drove for $\frac{2}{3}$ of an hour to visit her aunt and uncle. They then drove $\frac{1}{4}$ of an hour to attend a concert. What fraction of an hour did Arti's family spend in the car?

3. Remember that a number is divisible by 3 if the sum of its digits equals a multiple of three. Use this strategy to decide which of the following numbers are divisible by 3:

   A. 1083

   B. 748

   C. 1536

4. Edward lives $\frac{3}{5}$ of a mile from school, Brandon lives $\frac{7}{10}$ of a mile from school, and John lives $\frac{2}{3}$ of a mile from school.

   A. Which boy lives the farthest from school?

   B. Which boy lives the closest to school?

   C. Explain the strategies you used to answer Parts A and B.

5. Marcus likes to help his family with their work at the Good For You Bakery. He often packages cookies into dozens. Marcus had 6738 cookies to package into dozens on Saturday.

   A. How many dozens could Marcus package?

   B. What fraction of a dozen cookies did Marcus have left over?

   C. Write a reduced fraction for the fraction of a dozen left over.

From Factors to Fractions   SG • Grade 5 • Unit 11 • Lesson 8   **373**

Student Guide - page 373 *(Answers on p. 104)*

Teaching the Activity

This problem set can serve many purposes. It presents opportunities to choose appropriate methods to solve problems. You can use it as a supplement for homework or as an assessment. Assign some or all of the problems to reinforce certain concepts.

Question 1 involves an understanding of factors and the game *Factor 40* from Lesson 1. Encourage students to model the moves Romesh and John make as they solve this problem.

Questions 2 and *4* involve adding and subtracting fractions. Students can use any method to solve these problems including drawing rectangles, using a calculator, and finding common denominators. Encourage students to use estimates to check their work on these problems.

Question 3 reminds students of the divisibility rule for 3: if the sum of the digits is divisible by 3, then the number is divisible by 3.

In *Question 5,* there are 6 cookies remaining. Students should express the $\frac{6}{12}$ in lowest terms as $\frac{1}{2}$.

Homework and Practice

Assign some or all of the problems for homework.

At a Glance

Teaching the Activity

Students complete *Questions 1–5* on the *From Factors to Fractions* Activity Page in the *Student Guide*.

Homework

Assign some or all of the problems as homework.

Answer Key is on page 104.

Notes:

From Factors to Fractions

Complete each of the following problems. Show how you found each solution.

1. Romesh and John were playing *Factor 40* after school. John made the first move. He chose to circle 29.
   A. Was this a good first move? Explain the reasons for your answer.
   B. Was there a better first move? Explain your thinking.

2. Arti's family drove for $\frac{2}{3}$ of an hour to visit her aunt and uncle. They then drove $\frac{1}{4}$ of an hour to attend a concert. What fraction of an hour did Arti's family spend in the car?

3. Remember that a number is divisible by 3 if the sum of its digits equals a multiple of three. Use this strategy to decide which of the following numbers are divisible by 3:
   A. 1083
   B. 748
   C. 1536

4. Edward lives $\frac{5}{8}$ of a mile from school, Brandon lives $\frac{7}{10}$ of a mile from school, and John lives $\frac{2}{5}$ of a mile from school.
   A. Which boy lives the farthest from school?
   B. Which boy lives the closest to school?
   C. Explain the strategies you used to answer Parts A and B.

5. Marcus likes to help his family with their work at the Good For You Bakery. He often packages cookies into dozens. Marcus had 6738 cookies to package into dozens on Saturday.
   A. How many dozens could Marcus package?
   B. What fraction of a dozen cookies did Marcus have left over?
   C. Write a reduced fraction for the fraction of a dozen left over.

Student Guide - page 373

Student Guide (p. 373)

From Factors to Fractions

1. **A.** Yes; since 29 is a prime number John gets 29 points and Romesh only gets 1 point.

   B. A better choice is 31 or 37 because those are also prime numbers. John would get 31 or 37 points and Romesh would only get 1 point.

2. $\frac{2}{3} + \frac{1}{4} = \frac{11}{12}$ of an hour

3. **A.** The sum of the digits of 1083 is 12. Since 12 is divisible by 3, 1083 is also divisible by 3.

   B. The sum of the digits of 748 is 19. Since 19 is not divisible by 3, 748 is not divisible by 3.

   C. The sum of the digits of 1536 is 15. Since 15 is divisible by 3, 1536 is also divisible by 3.

4. **A.** Brandon

   B. John

   C. The common denominator for $\frac{5}{8}$, $\frac{7}{10}$, and $\frac{2}{5}$ is 40. $\frac{5}{8} = \frac{25}{40}$, $\frac{7}{10} = \frac{28}{40}$, and $\frac{2}{5} = \frac{16}{40}$. $\frac{16}{40} < \frac{25}{40} < \frac{28}{40}$. Therefore Brandon lives the farthest from school and John lives the closest to school.

5. **A.** 561

   B. $\frac{6}{12}$

   C. $\frac{1}{2}$

Discovery Assignment Book (pp. 177–178)

Part 1. Multiplication and Division Practice

1. A. 41 R38
   B. 1932
   C. 11,763
   D. 3201
2. Strategies will vary. One possible strategy is given for each.
   For 1A: $2000 \div 50 = 40$
   For 1C: Between
   $1000 \times 9 = 9000$ and
   $1300 \times 10 = 13{,}000$

Part 2. Going to the Theater

1. Friday–125, Saturday–144, Sunday–130
2. Friday–$1584, Saturday–$1771, Sunday–$1570
3. $320 - 79 = 241$

Part 3. Using Exponents

1. A. $180 = 2^2 \times 3^2 \times 5$
   B. $2125 = 5^3 \times 17$
   C. $17820 = 2^2 \times 3^4 \times 5 \times 11$
2. A. $20 = 5 \times 2 \times 2$
   $20 = 2^2 \times 5$

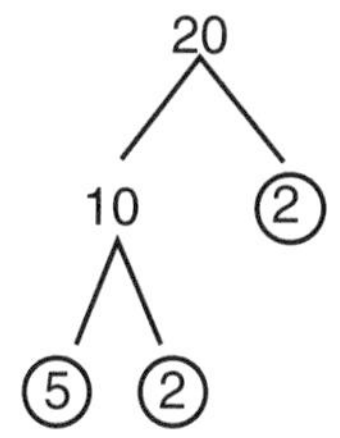

   B. $48 = 3 \times 2 \times 2 \times 2 \times 2$
   $48 = 2^4 \times 3$

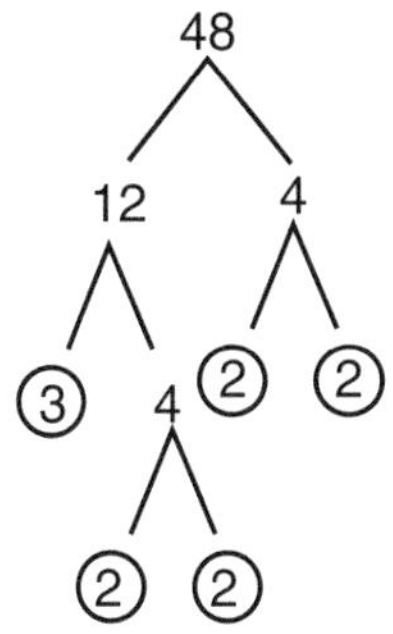

Name ______ Date ______

Unit 11 Home Practice

PART 1 Multiplication and Division Practice

Use paper and pencil to solve the following problems. Estimate to be sure your answers are reasonable.

1. A. $2170 \div 52 =$ B. $28 \times 69 =$
   C. $1307 \times 9 =$ D. $9603 \div 3 =$
2. Explain your estimation strategies for Questions 1A and 1C.

PART 2 Going to the Theater

Arti and Lin helped collect tickets at Arti's mother's theater. Tickets for the play are $14 for adults and $9 for students. Adult theater members get a discount and only have to pay half-price ($7).

Number of Tickets in Each Category

Performance	Adult Tickets (full price)	Student Tickets	Adult Member Tickets
Friday	97	15	13
Saturday	103	21	20
Sunday	82	43	5

1. How many people attended each performance of the play?
2. Find the amount of money collected for each performance.
3. How many more adults than students saw the play?

NUMBER PATTERNS, PRIMES, AND FRACTIONS DAB • Grade 5 • Unit 11 **177**

***Discovery Assignment Book* - page 177**

Name ______ Date ______

PART 3 Using Exponents

1. Each of the three numbers below is written as a product of primes. Rewrite the prime factorizations using exponents.
   A. $180 = 2 \times 3 \times 5 \times 2 \times 3 =$ ______
   B. $2125 = 5 \times 17 \times 5 \times 5 =$ ______
   C. $17{,}820 = 11 \times 2 \times 3 \times 3 \times 5 \times 2 \times 3 \times 3 =$ ______
2. Write each of the following numbers as a product of its primes without exponents. Use factor trees. Then write the number as a product of its primes using exponents.
   A. 20 B. 48 C. 56

PART 4 Fractions

1. Reduce the following fractions to lowest terms.
   A. $\frac{14}{28}$ B. $\frac{24}{42}$ C. $\frac{60}{200}$ D. $\frac{27}{90}$ E. $\frac{57}{120}$
2. Solve the following. First, find common denominators and then add or subtract. Reduce your answers to lowest terms.
   A. $\frac{4}{5} - \frac{3}{10} =$ B. $\frac{2}{5} - \frac{1}{15} =$ C. $\frac{5}{6} + \frac{1}{24} =$

178 DAB • Grade 5 • Unit 11 NUMBER PATTERNS, PRIMES, AND FRACTIONS

***Discovery Assignment Book* - page 178**

C. $56 = 2 \times 2 \times 2 \times 7$
$56 = 2^3 \times 7$

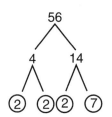

Part 4. Fractions

1. **A.** $\frac{1}{2}$

   B. $\frac{4}{7}$

   C. $\frac{3}{10}$

   D. $\frac{3}{10}$

   E. $\frac{19}{40}$

2. **A.** $\frac{5}{10} = \frac{1}{2}$

   B. $\frac{5}{15} = \frac{1}{3}$

   C. $\frac{21}{24} = \frac{7}{8}$

Name _____ Date _____

PART 5 Practicing Computation

1. Solve the following problems using paper and pencil. Estimate to be sure your answers are reasonable. Explain your estimation strategies.

   A. 46 × 23 =   **B.** 372 × 9 =

2. Solve the following problems using a paper-and-pencil method. Express quotients as mixed numbers.

   A. 3850 × 5 =   **B.** 2076 ÷ 9 =   **C.** 78 × 19 =

   D. 5945 + 6148 =   **E.** 9035 − 2747 =   **F.** 2703 ÷ 13 =

NUMBER PATTERNS, PRIMES, AND FRACTIONS   DAB • Grade 5 • Unit 11 **179**

Discovery Assignment Book - page 179

Discovery Assignment Book (p. 179)

Part 5. Practicing Computation

1. Estimation strategies will vary.

   A. 1058; $50 \times 20 = 1000$

   B. 3348. The answer will be less than 372×10 or 3720.

2. **A.** 19,250

   B. $230\frac{6}{9} = 230\frac{2}{3}$

   C. 1482

   D. 12,093

   E. 6288

   F. $207\frac{12}{13}$

Discovery Assignment Book (p. 180)

Part 6. The Band

1. About 2400 miles

2. $300

3. $6500 + $300 = $6800

4. **A.** 6000 people

   B. $30,000

   C. $30,000 − $6800 = $23,200

   D. $4640

   E. $232

Name _____ Date _____

PART 6 The Band

Choose an appropriate method to solve each of the following problems. For some questions you may need to find an exact answer, while for others you may only need an estimate. For each question, you may choose to use paper and pencil, mental math, or a calculator. Use a separate sheet of paper to explain how you solved each problem.

1. The Krinkles, a pop rock band from Chicago, recently toured the United States. Their tour van can travel about 12 miles on 1 gallon of gas. They bought about 200 gallons of gas on their tour. About how many miles did they travel?

2. If gas costs $1.50 per gallon, how much did the Krinkles spend on gas during their tour?

3. The Krinkles tour lasted 20 days. Each day the Krinkles budgeted $20 per person for food and $45 per person for a motel room. There are 5 members in the band. What was the total amount of money the band budgeted to spend on food, motel rooms, and gas?

4. On average, 300 people came to each of their concerts. Tickets were $5.00 per person at every concert.

   A. If they performed each of the 20 days of the tour, about how many people saw the Krinkles on tour?

   B. About how much money did they collect?

   C. After paying for gas, motels, and food, about how much money was left to pay the band?

   D. About how much did each member make?

   E. About how much did each band member make each day?

180 DAB • Grade 5 • Unit 11   NUMBER PATTERNS, PRIMES, AND FRACTIONS

Copyright © Kendall/Hunt Publishing Company

Discovery Assignment Book - page 180

Glossary

This glossary provides definitions of key vocabulary terms in the Grade 5 lessons. Locations of key vocabulary terms in the curriculum are included with each definition. Components Key: URG = *Unit Resource Guide* and SG = *Student Guide*.

A

Acute Angle (URG Unit 6; SG Unit 6)
An angle that measures less than 90°.

Acute Triangle (URG Unit 6 & Unit 15; SG Unit 6 & Unit 15)
A triangle that has only acute angles.

All-Partials Multiplication Method (URG Unit 2)
A paper-and-pencil method for solving multiplication problems. Each partial product is recorded on a separate line. (*See also* partial product.)

$$\begin{array}{r} 186 \\ \times\ 3 \\ \hline 18 \\ 240 \\ 300 \\ \hline 558 \end{array}$$

Altitude of a Triangle (URG Unit 15; SG Unit 15)
A line segment from a vertex of a triangle perpendicular to the opposite side or to the line extending the opposite side; also, the length of this line. The altitude is also called the height of the triangle.

Angle (URG Unit 6; SG Unit 6)
The amount of turning or the amount of opening between two rays that have the same endpoint.

Arc (URG Unit 14; SG Unit 14)
Part of a circle between two points. (*See also* circle.)

Area (URG Unit 4 & Unit 15; SG Unit 4 & Unit 15)
A measurement of size. The area of a shape is the amount of space it covers, measured in square units.

Average (URG Unit 1 & Unit 4; SG Unit 1 & Unit 4)
A number that can be used to represent a typical value in a set of data. (*See also* mean, median, and mode.)

Axes (URG Unit 10; SG Unit 10)
Reference lines on a graph. In the Cartesian coordinate system, the axes are two perpendicular lines that meet at the origin. The singular of axes is axis.

B

Base of a Triangle (URG Unit 15; SG Unit 15)
One of the sides of a triangle; also, the length of the side. A perpendicular line drawn from the vertex opposite the base is called the height or altitude of the triangle.

Base of an Exponent (URG Unit 2; SG Unit 2)
When exponents are used, the number being multiplied. In $3^4 = 3 \times 3 \times 3 \times 3 = 81$, the 3 is the base and the 4 is the exponent. The 3 is multiplied by itself 4 times.

Base-Ten Pieces (URG Unit 2; SG Unit 2)
A set of manipulatives used to model our number system as shown in the figure below. Note that a skinny is made of 10 bits, a flat is made of 100 bits, and a pack is made of 1000 bits.

Base-Ten Shorthand (URG Unit 2)
A graphical representation of the base-ten pieces as shown below.

Nickname	Picture	Shorthand
bit		•
skinny		/
flat		
pack		

Benchmarks (SG Unit 7)
Numbers convenient for comparing and ordering numbers, e.g., $0, \frac{1}{2}, 1$ are convenient benchmarks for comparing and ordering fractions.

Best-Fit Line (URG Unit 3; SG Unit 3)
The line that comes closest to the points on a point graph.

Binning Data (URG Unit 8; SG Unit 8)
Placing data from a data set with a large number of values or large range into intervals in order to more easily see patterns in the data.

Bit (URG Unit 2; SG Unit 2)
A cube that measures 1 cm on each edge.
It is the smallest of the base-ten pieces and is often used to represent 1. (*See also* base-ten pieces.)

C

Cartesian Coordinate System (URG Unit 10; SG Unit 10)
A method of locating points on a flat surface by means of an ordered pair of numbers. This method is named after its originator, René Descartes. (*See also* coordinates.)

Categorical Variable (URG Unit 1; SG Unit 1)
Variables with values that are not numbers. (*See also* variable and value.)

Center of a Circle (URG Unit 14; SG Unit 14)
The point such that every point on a circle is the same distance from it. (*See also* circle.)

Centiwheel (URG Unit 7; SG Unit 7)
A circle divided into 100 equal sections used in exploring fractions, decimals, and percents.

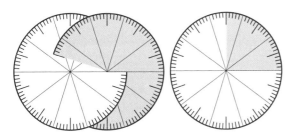

Central Angle (URG Unit 14; SG Unit 14)
An angle whose vertex is at the center of a circle.

Certain Event (URG Unit 7; SG Unit 7)
An event that has a probability of 1 (100%).

Chord (URG Unit 14; SG Unit 14)
A line segment that connects two points on a circle. (*See also* circle.)

Circle (URG Unit 14; SG Unit 14)
A curve that is made up of all the points that are the same distance from one point, the center.

Circumference (URG Unit 14; SG Unit 14)
The distance around a circle.

Common Denominator (URG Unit 5 & Unit 11; SG Unit 5 & Unit 11)
A denominator that is shared by two or more fractions. A common denominator is a common multiple of the denominators of the fractions. 15 is a common denominator of $\frac{2}{3}$ ($= \frac{10}{15}$) and $\frac{4}{5}$ ($= \frac{12}{15}$) since 15 is divisible by both 3 and 5.

Common Fraction (URG Unit 7; SG Unit 7)
Any fraction that is written with a numerator and denominator that are whole numbers. For example, $\frac{3}{4}$ and $\frac{9}{4}$ are both common fractions. (*See also* decimal fraction.)

Commutative Property of Addition (URG Unit 2)
The order of the addends in an addition problem does not matter, e.g., $7 + 3 = 3 + 7$.

Commutative Property of Multiplication (URG Unit 2)
The order of the factors in a multiplication problem does not matter, e.g., $7 \times 3 = 3 \times 7$. (*See also* turn-around facts.)

Compact Method (URG Unit 2)
Another name for what is considered the traditional multiplication algorithm.

$$\begin{array}{r} \overset{2\;1}{186} \\ \times\ 3 \\ \hline 558 \end{array}$$

Composite Number (URG Unit 11; SG Unit 11)
A number that has more than two distinct factors. For example, 9 has three factors (1, 3, 9) so it is a composite number.

Concentric Circles (URG Unit 14; SG Unit 14)
Circles that have the same center.

Congruent (URG Unit 6 & Unit 10; SG Unit 6)
Figures that are the same shape and size. Polygons are congruent when corresponding sides have the same length and corresponding angles have the same measure.

Conjecture (URG Unit 11; SG Unit 11)
A statement that has not been proved to be true, nor shown to be false.

Convenient Number (URG Unit 2; SG Unit 2)
A number used in computation that is close enough to give a good estimate, but is also easy to compute with mentally, e.g., 25 and 30 are convenient numbers for 27.

Convex (URG Unit 6)
A shape is convex if for any two points in the shape, the line segment between the points is also inside the shape.

Coordinates (URG Unit 10; SG Unit 10)
An ordered pair of numbers that locates points on a flat surface relative to a pair of coordinate axes. For example, in the ordered pair (4, 5), the first number (coordinate) is the distance from the point to the vertical axis and the second coordinate is the distance from the point to the horizontal axis. (*See also* axes.)

Corresponding Parts (URG Unit 10; SG Unit 10)
Matching parts in two or more figures. In the figure
below, Sides AB and A′B′ are corresponding parts.

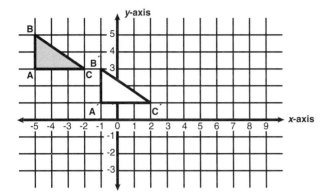

Cryptography (SG Unit 11) The study of secret codes.

Cubic Centimeter (URG Unit 13)
The volume of a cube that is one centimeter long on
each edge.

D

Data (SG Unit 1)
Information collected in an experiment or survey.

Decagon (URG Unit 6; SG Unit 6)
A ten-sided, ten-angled polygon.

Decimal (URG Unit 7; SG Unit 7)
1. A number written using the base ten place value
   system.
2. A number containing a decimal point.

Decimal Fraction (URG Unit 7; SG Unit 7)
A fraction written as a decimal. For example, 0.75 and
0.4 are decimal fractions and $\frac{75}{100}$ and $\frac{4}{10}$ are the equivalent
common fractions.

Degree (URG Unit 6; SG Unit 6)
A degree (°) is a unit of measure for angles. There are
360 degrees in a circle.

Denominator (URG Unit 3; SG Unit 3)
The number below the line in a fraction. The denominator indicates the number of equal parts in which the unit
whole is divided. For example, the 5 is the denominator
in the fraction $\frac{2}{5}$. In this case the unit whole is divided into
five equal parts. (*See also* numerator.)

Density (URG Unit 13; SG Unit 13)
The ratio of an object's mass to its volume.

Diagonal (URG Unit 6)
A line segment that connects nonadjacent corners of
a polygon.

Diameter (URG Unit 14; SG Unit 14)
1. A line segment that connects two points on a circle
   and passes through the center.
2. The length of this line segment.

Digit (SG Unit 2)
Any one of the ten symbols 0, 1, 2, 3, 4, 5, 6, 7, 8, 9.
The number 37 is made up of the digits 3 and 7.

Dividend (URG Unit 4 & Unit 9; SG Unit 4 & Unit 9)
The number that is divided in a division problem,
e.g., 12 is the dividend in 12 ÷ 3 = 4.

Divisor (URG Unit 2, Unit 4, & Unit 9; SG Unit 2,
    Unit 4, & Unit 9)
In a division problem, the number by which another
number is divided. In the problem 12 ÷ 4 = 3, the 4
is the divisor, the 12 is the dividend, and the 3 is the
quotient.

Dodecagon (URG Unit 6; SG Unit 6)
A twelve-sided, twelve-angled polygon.

E

Endpoint (URG Unit 6; SG Unit 6)
The point at either end of a line segment or the point at
the end of a ray.

Equally Likely (URG Unit 7; SG Unit 7)
When events have the same probability, they are called
equally likely.

Equidistant (URG Unit 14)
At the same distance.

Equilateral Triangle (URG Unit 6, Unit 14, & Unit 15)
A triangle that has all three sides equal in length. An
equilateral triangle also has three equal angles.

Equivalent Fractions (URG Unit 3; SG Unit 3)
Fractions that have the same value, e.g., $\frac{2}{4} = \frac{1}{2}$.

Estimate (URG Unit 2; SG Unit 2)
1. To find *about* how many (as a verb).
2. A number that is *close to* the desired number (as a
   noun).

Expanded Form (SG Unit 2)
A way to write numbers that shows the place value of
each digit, e.g., 4357 = 4000 + 300 + 50 + 7.

Exponent (URG Unit 2 & Unit 11; SG Unit 2 & Unit 11)
The number of times the base is multiplied by itself.
In $3^4 = 3 \times 3 \times 3 \times 3 = 81$, the 3 is the base and the
4 is the exponent. The 3 is multiplied by itself 4 times.

Extrapolation (URG Unit 13; SG Unit 13)
Using patterns in data to make predictions or to estimate
values that lie beyond the range of values in the set of
data.

F

Fact Families (URG Unit 2; SG Unit 2)
Related math facts, e.g., 3 × 4 = 12, 4 × 3 = 12,
12 ÷ 3 = 4, 12 ÷ 4 = 3.

Factor Tree (URG Unit 11; SG Unit 11)
A diagram that shows the prime factorization of a number.

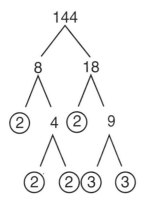

Factors (URG Unit 2 & Unit 11; SG Unit 2 & Unit 11)
1. In a multiplication problem, the numbers that are multiplied together. In the problem $3 \times 4 = 12$, 3 and 4 are the factors.
2. Numbers that divide a number evenly, e.g., 1, 2, 3, 4, 6, and 12 are all the factors of 12.

Fair Game (URG Unit 7; SG Unit 7)
A game in which it is equally likely that any player will win.

Fewest Pieces Rule (URG Unit 2)
Using the least number of base-ten pieces to represent a number. (*See also* base-ten pieces.)

Fixed Variables (URG Unit 4; SG Unit 3 & Unit 4)
Variables in an experiment that are held constant or not changed, in order to find the relationship between the manipulated and responding variables. These variables are often called controlled variables. (*See also* manipulated variable and responding variable.)

Flat (URG Unit 2; SG Unit 2)
A block that measures 1 cm × 10 cm × 10 cm. It is one of the base-ten pieces and is often used to represent 100. (*See also* base-ten pieces.)

Flip (URG Unit 10; SG Unit 10)
A motion of the plane in which the plane is reflected over a line so that any point and its image are the same distance from the line.

Forgiving Division Method
(URG Unit 4; SG Unit 4)
A paper-and-pencil method for division in which successive partial quotients are chosen and subtracted from the dividend, until the remainder is less than the divisor. The sum of the partial quotients is the quotient. For example, 644 ÷ 7 can be solved as shown at the right.

$$
\begin{array}{r}
92 \\
7\overline{)644} \\
\underline{140} \;|\; 20 \\
504 \\
\underline{350} \;|\; 50 \\
154 \\
\underline{140} \;|\; 20 \\
14 \\
\underline{14} \;|\; 2 \\
0 \;|\; 92
\end{array}
$$

Formula (SG Unit 11 & Unit 14)
A number sentence that gives a general rule. A formula for finding the area of a rectangle is Area = length × width, or $A = l \times w$.

Fraction (URG Unit 7; SG Unit 7)
A number that can be written as a/b where a and b are whole numbers and b is not zero.

G

Googol (URG Unit 2)
A number that is written as a 1 with 100 zeroes after it (10^{100}).

Googolplex (URG Unit 2)
A number that is written as a 1 with a googol of zeroes after it.

H

Height of a Triangle (URG Unit 15; SG Unit 15)
A line segment from a vertex of a triangle perpendicular to the opposite side or to the line extending the opposite side; also, the length of this line. The height is also called the altitude.

Hexagon (URG Unit 6; SG Unit 6)
A six-sided polygon.

Hypotenuse (URG Unit 15; SG Unit 15)
The longest side of a right triangle.

I

Image (URG Unit 10; SG Unit 10)
The result of a transformation, in particular a slide (translation) or a flip (reflection), in a coordinate plane. The new figure after the slide or flip is the image of the old figure.

Impossible Event (URG Unit 7; SG Unit 7)
An event that has a probability of 0 or 0%.

Improper Fraction (URG Unit 3; SG Unit 3)
A fraction in which the numerator is greater than or equal to the denominator. An improper fraction is greater than or equal to one.

Infinite (URG Unit 2)
Never ending, immeasurably great, unlimited.

Interpolation (URG Unit 13; SG Unit 13)
Making predictions or estimating values that lie between data points in a set of data.

Intersect (URG Unit 14)
To meet or cross.

Isosceles Triangle (URG Unit 6 & Unit 15)
A triangle that has at least two sides of equal length.

J

K

L

Lattice Multiplication
(URG Unit 9; SG Unit 9)
A method for multiplying that uses a lattice to arrange the partial products so the digits are correctly placed in the correct place value columns. A lattice for $43 \times 96 = 4128$ is shown at the right.

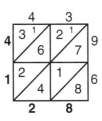

Legs of a Right Triangle (URG Unit 15; SG Unit 15)
The two sides of a right triangle that form the right angle.

Length of a Rectangle (URG Unit 4 & Unit 15; SG Unit 4 & Unit 15)
The distance along one side of a rectangle.

Line
A set of points that form a straight path extending infinitely in two directions.

Line of Reflection (URG Unit 10)
A line that acts as a mirror so that after a shape is flipped over the line, corresponding points are at the same distance (equidistant) from the line.

Line Segment (URG Unit 14)
A part of a line between and including two points, called the endpoints.

Liter (URG Unit 13)
Metric unit used to measure volume. A liter is a little more than a quart.

Lowest Terms (SG Unit 11)
A fraction is in lowest terms if the numerator and denominator have no common factor greater than 1.

M

Manipulated Variable (URG Unit 4; SG Unit 4)
In an experiment, the variable with values known at the beginning of the experiment. The experimenter often chooses these values before data is collected. The manipulated variable is often called the independent variable.

Mass (URG Unit 13)
The amount of matter in an object.

Mean (URG Unit 1 & Unit 4; SG Unit 1 & Unit 4)
An average of a set of numbers that is found by adding the values of the data and dividing by the number of values.

Measurement Division (URG Unit 4)
Division as equal grouping. The total number of objects and the number of objects in each group are known. The number of groups is the unknown. For example, tulip bulbs come in packages of 8. If 216 bulbs are sold, how many packages are sold?

Median (URG Unit 1; SG Unit 1)
For a set with an odd number of data arranged in order, it is the middle number. For an even number of data arranged in order, it is the mean of the two middle numbers.

Meniscus (URG Unit 13)
The curved surface formed when a liquid creeps up the side of a container (for example, a graduated cylinder).

Milliliter (ml) (URG Unit 13)
A measure of capacity in the metric system that is the volume of a cube that is one centimeter long on each side.

Mixed Number (URG Unit 3; SG Unit 3)
A number that is written as a whole number followed by a fraction. It is equal to the sum of the whole number and the fraction.

Mode (URG Unit 1; SG Unit 1)
The most common value in a data set.

Mr. Origin (URG Unit 10; SG Unit 10)
A plastic figure used to represent the origin of a coordinate system and to indicate the directions of the x- and y- axes. (and possibly the z-axis).

N

N-gon (URG Unit 6; SG Unit 6)
A polygon with N sides.

Negative Number (URG Unit 10; SG Unit 10)
A number less than zero; a number to the left of zero on a horizontal number line.

Nonagon (URG Unit 6; SG Unit 6)
A nine-sided polygon.

Numerator (URG Unit 3; SG Unit 3)
The number written above the line in a fraction. For example, the 2 is the numerator in the fraction $\frac{2}{5}$. In this case, we are interested in two of the five parts. (*See also* denominator.)

Numerical Expression (URG Unit 4; SG Unit 4)
A combination of numbers and operations, e.g., $5 + 8 \div 4$.

Numerical Variable (URG Unit 1; SG Unit 1)
Variables with values that are numbers. (*See also* variable and value.)

O

Obtuse Angle (URG Unit 6; SG Unit 6)
An angle that measures more than 90°.

Obtuse Triangle (URG Unit 6 & Unit 15; SG Unit 6 & Unit 15)
A triangle that has an obtuse angle.

Octagon (URG Unit 6; SG Unit 6)
An eight-sided polygon.

Ordered Pair (URG Unit 10; SG Unit 10)
A pair of numbers that gives the coordinates of a point on a grid in relation to the origin. The horizontal coordinate is given first; the vertical coordinate is given second. For example, the ordered pair (5, 3) gives the coordinates of the point that is 5 units to the right of the origin and 3 units up.

Origin (URG Unit 10; SG Unit 10)
The point at which the *x*- and *y*-axes intersect on a coordinate plane. The origin is described by the ordered pair (0, 0) and serves as a reference point so that all the points on the plane can be located by ordered pairs.

P

Pack (URG Unit 2; SG Unit 2)
A cube that measures 10 cm on each edge. It is one of the base-ten pieces and is often used to represent 1000. (*See also* base-ten pieces.)

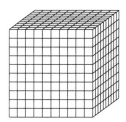

Parallel Lines
(URG Unit 6 & Unit 10)
Lines that are in the same direction. In the plane, parallel lines are lines that do not intersect.

Parallelogram (URG Unit 6)
A quadrilateral with two pairs of parallel sides.

Partial Product (URG Unit 2)
One portion of the multiplication process in the all-partials multiplication method, e.g., in the problem 3 × 186 there are three partial products: 3 × 6 = <u>18</u>, 3 × 80 = <u>240</u>, and 3 × 100 = <u>300</u>. (*See also* all-partials multiplication method.)

Partitive Division (URG Unit 4)
Division as equal sharing. The total number of objects and the number of groups are known. The number of objects in each group is the unknown. For example, Frank has 144 marbles that he divides equally into 6 groups. How many marbles are in each group?

Pentagon (URG Unit 6; SG Unit 6)
A five-sided polygon.

Percent (URG Unit 7; SG Unit 7)
Per hundred or out of 100. A special ratio that compares a number to 100. For example, 20% (twenty percent) of the jelly beans are yellow means that out of every 100 jelly beans, 20 are yellow.

Perimeter (URG Unit 15; SG Unit 15)
The distance around a two-dimensional shape.

Period (SG Unit 2)
A group of three places in a large number, starting on the right, often separated by commas as shown at the right.

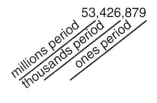

Perpendicular Lines (URG Unit 14 & Unit 15; SG Unit 14)
Lines that meet at right angles.

Pi (π) (URG Unit 14; SG Unit 14)
The ratio of the circumference to diameter of a circle. π = 3.14159265358979. . . . It is a nonterminating, nonrepeating decimal.

Place (SG Unit 2)
The position of a digit in a number.

Place Value (URG Unit 2; SG Unit 2)
The value of a digit in a number. For example, the 5 is in the hundreds place in 4573, so it stands for 500.

Polygon (URG Unit 6; SG Unit 6)
A two-dimensional connected figure made of line segments in which each endpoint of every side meets with an endpoint of exactly one other side.

Population (URG Unit 1 Unit 1)
A collection of persons or things whose properties will be analyzed in a survey or experiment.

Portfolio (URG Unit 2; SG Unit 2)
A collection of student work that show how a student's skills, attitudes, and knowledge change over time.

Positive Number (URG Unit 10; SG Unit 10)
A number greater than zero; a number to the right of zero on a horizontal number line.

Power (URG Unit 2; SG Unit 2)
An exponent. Read 10^4 as, "ten to the fourth power" or "ten to the fourth." We say 10,000 or 10^4 is the fourth power of ten.

Prime Factorization (URG Unit 11; SG Unit 11)
Writing a number as a product of primes. The prime factorization of 100 is 2 × 2 × 5 × 5.

Prime Number (URG Unit 11; SG Unit 11)
A number that has exactly two factors: itself and 1. For example, 7 has exactly two distinct factors, 1 and 7.

Probability (URG Unit 7; SG Unit 1 & Unit 7)
A number from 0 to 1 (0% to 100%) that describes how likely an event is to happen. The closer that the probability of an event is to one, the more likely the event will happen.

Product (URG Unit 2; SG Unit 2)
The answer to a multiplication problem. In the problem $3 \times 4 = 12$, 12 is the product.

Proper Fraction (URG Unit 3; SG Unit 3)
A fraction in which the numerator is less than the denominator. Proper fractions are less than one.

Proportion (URG Unit 3 & Unit 13; SG Unit 13)
A statement that two ratios are equal.

Protractor (URG Unit 6; SG Unit 6)
A tool for measuring angles.

Q

Quadrants (URG Unit 10; SG Unit 10)
The four sections of a coordinate grid that are separated by the axes.

Quadrilateral (URG Unit 6; SG Unit 6)
A polygon with four sides. (*See also* polygon.)

Quotient (URG Unit 4 & Unit 9; SG Unit 2, Unit 4, & Unit 9)
The answer to a division problem. In the problem $12 \div 3 = 4$, the 4 is the quotient.

R

Radius (URG Unit 14; SG Unit 14)
1. A line segment connecting the center of a circle to any point on the circle.
2. The length of this line segment.

Ratio (URG Unit 3 & Unit 12; SG Unit 3 & Unit 13)
A way to compare two numbers or quantities using division. It is often written as a fraction.

Ray (URG Unit 6; SG Unit 6)
A part of a line with one endpoint that extends indefinitely in one direction.

Rectangle (URG Unit 6; SG Unit 6)
A quadrilateral with four right angles.

Reflection (URG Unit 10)
(*See* flip.)

Regular Polygon (URG Unit 6; SG Unit 6; DAB Unit 6)
A polygon with all sides of equal length and all angles equal.

Remainder (URG Unit 4 & Unit 9; SG Unit 4 & Unit 9)
Something that remains or is left after a division problem. The portion of the dividend that is not evenly divisible by the divisor, e.g., $16 \div 5 = 3$ with 1 as a remainder.

Repeating Decimals (SG Unit 9)
A decimal fraction with one or more digits repeating without end.

Responding Variable (URG Unit 4; SG Unit 4)
The variable whose values result from the experiment. Experimenters find the values of the responding variable by doing the experiment. The responding variable is often called the dependent variable.

Rhombus (URG Unit 6; SG Unit 6)
A quadrilateral with four equal sides.

Right Angle (URG Unit 6; SG Unit 6)
An angle that measures 90°.

Right Triangle (URG Unit 6 & Unit 15; SG Unit 6 & Unit 15)
A triangle that contains a right angle.

Rubric (URG Unit 1)
A scoring guide that can be used to guide or assess student work.

S

Sample (URG Unit 1)
A part or subset of a population.

Scalene Triangle (URG Unit 15)
A triangle that has no sides that are equal in length.

Scientific Notation (URG Unit 2; SG Unit 2)
A way of writing numbers, particularly very large or very small numbers. A number in scientific notation has two factors. The first factor is a number greater than or equal to one and less than ten. The second factor is a power of 10 written with an exponent. For example, 93,000,000 written in scientific notation is 9.3×10^7.

Septagon (URG Unit 6; SG Unit 6)
A seven-sided polygon.

Side-Angle-Side (URG Unit 6 & Unit 14)
A geometric property stating that two triangles having two corresponding sides with the included angle equal are congruent.

Side-Side-Side (URG Unit 6)
A geometric property stating that two triangles having corresponding sides equal are congruent.

Sides of an Angle (URG Unit 6; SG Unit 6)
The sides of an angle are two rays with the same endpoint. (*See also* endpoint and ray.)

Sieve of Eratosthenes (SG Unit 11)
A method for separating prime numbers from nonprime numbers developed by Eratosthenes, an Egyptian librarian, in about 240 BCE.

Similar (URG Unit 6; SG Unit 6)
Similar shapes have the same shape but not necessarily the same size.

Skinny (URG Unit 2; SG Unit 2)
A block that measures 1 cm × 1 cm × 10 cm.
It is one of the base-ten pieces
and is often used to represent 10.
(*See also* base-ten pieces.)

Slide (URG Unit 10; SG Unit 10)
Moving a geometric figure in the plane by moving every point of the figure the same distance in the same direction. Also called translation.

Speed (URG Unit 3 & Unit 5; SG Unit 3 & Unit 5)
The ratio of distance moved to time taken, e.g.,
3 miles/1 hour or 3 mph is a speed.

Square (URG Unit 6 & Unit 14; SG Unit 6)
A quadrilateral with four equal sides and four right angles.

Square Centimeter (URG Unit 4; SG Unit 4)
The area of a square that is 1 cm long on each side.

Square Number (URG Unit 11)
A number that is the product of a whole number multiplied by itself. For example, 25 is a square number since $5 \times 5 = 25$. A square number can be represented by a square array with the same number of rows as columns. A square array for 25 has 5 rows of 5 objects in each row or 25 total objects.

Standard Form (SG Unit 2)
The traditional way to write a number, e.g., standard form for three hundred fifty-seven is 357. (*See also* expanded form and word form.)

Standard Units (URG Unit 4)
Internationally or nationally agreed-upon units used in measuring variables, e.g., centimeters and inches are standard units used to measure length and square centimeters and square inches are used to measure area.

Straight Angle (URG Unit 6; SG Unit 6)
An angle that measures 180º.

T

Ten Percent (URG Unit 4; SG Unit 4)
10 out of every hundred or $\frac{1}{10}$.

Tessellation (URG Unit 6 & Unit 10; SG Unit 6)
A pattern made up of one or more repeated shapes that completely covers a surface without any gaps or overlaps.

Translation
(*See* slide.)

Trapezoid (URG Unit 6)
A quadrilateral with exactly one pair of parallel sides.

Triangle (URG Unit 6; SG Unit 6)
A polygon with three sides.

Triangulating (URG Unit 6; SG Unit 6)
Partitioning a polygon into two or more nonoverlapping triangles by drawing diagonals that do not intersect.

Turn-Around Facts (URG Unit 2)
Multiplication facts that have the same factors but in a different order, e.g., $3 \times 4 = 12$ and $4 \times 3 = 12$. (*See also* commutative property of multiplication.)

Twin Primes (URG Unit 11; SG Unit 11)
A pair of prime numbers whose difference is 2. For example, 3 and 5 are twin primes.

U

Unit Ratio (URG Unit 13; SG Unit 13)
A ratio with a denominator of one.

V

Value (URG Unit 1; SG Unit 1)
The possible outcomes of a variable. For example, red, green, and blue are possible values for the variable *color*. Two meters and 1.65 meters are possible values for the variable *length*.

Variable (URG Unit 1; SG Unit 1)
1. An attribute or quantity that changes or varies.
   (*See also* categorical variable and numerical variable.)
2. A symbol that can stand for a variable.

Variables in Proportion (URG Unit 13; SG Unit 13)
When the ratio of two variables in an experiment is always the same, the variables are in proportion.

Velocity (URG Unit 5; SG Unit 5)
Speed in a given direction. Speed is the ratio of the distance traveled to time taken.

Vertex (URG Unit 6; SG Unit 6)
A common point of two rays or line segments that form an angle.

Volume (URG Unit 13)
The measure of the amount of space occupied by an object.

W

Whole Number
Any of the numbers 0, 1, 2, 3, 4, 5, 6 and so on.

Width of a Rectangle (URG Unit 4 & Unit 15; SG Unit 4 & Unit 15)
The distance along one side of a rectangle is the length and the distance along an adjacent side is the width.

Word Form (SG Unit 2)
A number expressed in words, e.g., the word form for 123 is "one hundred twenty-three." (*See also* expanded form and standard form.)

X

Y

Z